VALUES, ATTITUDES AND BEHAVIOUR CHANGE

Ben Reich and Christine Adcock

Methuen

In memory of my parents
Mordechai and Rebecca Reich

B.R.

First published in 1976 by Methuen & Co Ltd
11 New Fetter Lane, London EC4P 4EE
© 1976 Ben Reich and Christine Adcock
Printed in Great Britain by
Richard Clay (The Chaucer Press) Ltd
Bungay, Suffolk

ISBN hardback 416 82760 8
ISBN paperback 416 82770 5

We are grateful to Grant McIntyre of
Open Books Publishing Ltd
for assistance in the preparation of this series

This book is available in both hardbound and paperback editions. The paperback edition is sold subject to the condition that it shall not, by way of trade or otherwise, be lent, resold, hired out or otherwise circulated without the publisher's prior consent in any form of binding or cover other than that in which it is published and without a similar condition including this condition being imposed on the subsequent purchaser.

E8342/2

GLASGOW UNIVERSITY DEPARTMENTAL LIBRARIES

Contents

Editor's Introduction

How central a part of ourselves are our attitudes? Ben Reich and Christine Adcock suggest that they are closely related to the underlying values by which we judge our experiences. They suggest that any effort to change attitudes must take a person's values into account. Fortunately for our self-esteem, they show that our ability to resist such attempts is considerable. Furthermore, they stress the indirect relationship between a person's attitudes and the behaviour he actually adopts in particular social situations.

Values, Attitudes and Behaviour Change belongs to Unit B of *Essential Psychology*. What unifies the books in this unit is their subject matter; all deal with the individual in society. In order to cope adequately with their findings, social psychologists have had to develop different conceptual frameworks. The analogy of a human being as a computer (employed in Unit A) may be appropriate, perhaps, to some one-to-one interpersonal situations. But to do justice to what happens in groups, new concepts (e.g. role) and new models (e.g. dynamic models) have been more useful. The reader will find other general conceptual frameworks in other units. They are not so much mutually contradictory as efforts to do justice to the complexities of psychology's subject matter. Living with a variety of explanatory frameworks decreases our confidence in psychology as a mature science; but perhaps it is better to be honest about what we don't know.

Essential Psychology as a whole is designed to reflect the changing structure and function of psychology. The authors are both academic and professionals, and their aim has been to introduce the most important concepts in their areas to beginning students. They have tried to do so clearly but have not attempted to conceal the fact that concepts that now appear central to their work may soon be peripheral. In other words, they have presented psychology as a developing set of views of man, not as a body of received truth. Readers are not intended to study the whole series in order to 'master the basics'. Rather, since different people may wish to use different theoretical frameworks for their own purposes, the series has been designed so that each title stands on its own. But it is possible that if the reader has read no psychology before, he will enjoy individual books more if he has read the introductions (A1, B1, etc.) to the units to which they belong. Readers of the units concerned with applications of psychology (E, F) may benefit from reading all the introductions.

A word about references in the text to the work of other writers – e.g. 'Smith, 1974'. These occur where the author feels he must acknowledge (by name) an important concept or some crucial evidence. The book or article referred to will be listed in the references (which double as name index) at the back of the book. The reader is invited to consult these sources if he wishes to explore topics further.

We hope you enjoy psychology.

Peter Herriot

I
Introduction

The study of psychology is in general, not the prerogative of the psychologist. Every person is trying to make sense of other people's and his own behaviour. He is looking for explanations of actions, and wondering *why* certain behaviour patterns seem to go together while others do not, and how it is possible for him to predict his own and other people's reactions. These issues are probably not unlike the questions asked by psychologists, however difficult the language and terminology which they employ. This general interest is even more likely to be the case when we look at the range of problems that are of special interest to the social psychologist. This is so because our whole life is coloured by some social interaction, our current behaviour is often influenced by our relationships with other people, or by anticipated future interactions with them. Even our private thoughts are frequently about others or are seen in relation to others: i.e. 'what they would think'. Furthermore, our present behaviour is frequently constrained by specific role interactions: being a member of a trade union or talking as a doctor to other doctors. In these cases our roles impose certain ways of behaving, and when we are in the company of others who occupy similar roles, they expect the same of us. Lastly, our present behaviour is strongly influenced, if not actually determined, by our past interactions with others.

It is, of course, true that much of our interaction has become habitual and does not require our continuous monitoring or understanding. But as soon as people, or we ourselves, fail to behave in the expected way, or behave oddly, we have to 'make sense' of this, or 'reorientate' to it.

It can also be argued that psychologists researching in this area utilize our common interest in these questions. Original hypotheses often start with an observation or intuitive hunch, based on self observation or the observation of others. The researcher, if he is interested in experimental procedures (see *Essential Psychology*, A8) will then attempt to isolate that particular factor (independent variable) which he believes to be the *cause* for the observed behaviour (dependent variable). He will often do this by varying the stimuli, and thereby hope to show that the causal link with a particular behaviour pattern holds true only for his postulated stimulus.

He may, on the other hand, be aware that more than one factor is responsible for the behaviour. The experimenter will then attempt to tease out the relative importance of each factor. Let us illustrate this with an example. We have a notion that people prefer those who are similar to themselves (positive attitude) and dislike those who are dissimilar to themselves (negative attitude). For example, some whites dislike Negroes, and the dissimilarities that they notice range from colour of skin and type of face structure, to beliefs and attitudes on a variety of topics. Which is the more important factor in determining the dislike – the racial or ideological differences?

Let us now give a test to a variety of individuals on which they can indicate degrees of liking and disliking. It is now feasible to devise an imaginary person with any variety of attributes. For example, the person is described as white middle class American with strange attitudes. Or he is black and has beliefs similar to yours. By varying the imaginary person in different ways we should be able to find which attributes most determine whether he is liked or disliked. For instance, a white rater might like the black person with similar attitudes to his own more than the white person with different attitudes, thus demonstrating that attitudes were a more important attribute to him than skin colour. This example is in fact a simplified version of an experiment carried out by Rokeach and Mezei (1966). Their investigations revealed that subjects, even anti-Negro whites, preferred those whose beliefs are similar to theirs, rather than those whose colour is the same but whose beliefs differ. It therefore appears that shared attitudes and beliefs may play an important role in perceived similarity, which itself contributes to interpersonal attraction.

You may find that some of the conclusions reached by psychologists appear to be obvious. In view of what was said earlier this should not be surprising. You may not have thought of the results before you read them; and this is often forgotten. *After* reading them, you may think 'of course this makes sense'. Our point is that it *ought* to make sense, because the basic fodder of the researcher is our shared daily behaviour. Our culture in general and our experience as individuals have taught us ways of connecting psychological and behavioural phenomena. Unfortunately, many psychologists persist in patronizing others by calling them 'laymen' and ignoring their psychological insights.

Another point to bear in mind: a theory is not just concerned with explaining one discrete connection between two events, but attempts to tie together a number of results which can be explained by the theory. Furthermore the psychologist will make predictions on the basis of that theory about what should happen if a new factor is introduced.

Much of what we have mentioned so far is true for psychology in general, but perhaps most of all in the area which is the concern of this book. The study of *attitudes* holds a central position within the domain of social psychology. It is easy to see why. We are not born with them, nor are they attributed to physiological maturation. Attitudes are thus acquired or learnt. Since we all have attitudes there must be some *need* to acquire them because of some function which they serve. What is the need? Could we do without them? Furthermore, when we possess an attitude related to some object or person, although it is subject to changes, it has a fixed quality about it; it seems to be enduring rather than temporary. What maintains the stability of such an attitude? And finally, if we want to change someone's attitude, or for that matter our own, what is the best way to do so? These are some of the questions psychologists have asked themselves with reference to attitudes.

The title of the book also includes the terms *values* and *behaviour change*. A moment's consideration of the terms values and attitudes makes one realize that, though the two are related, they are not synonymous. Values are less specific than attitudes. Having an attitude implies the existence of some object towards which one has it. This is not the case with values, whether they refer for instance to security, peace of mind, or honesty. Another important distinction between values and attitudes is that values serve as standards; one can view them as ideals for which we strive. From this point of view, attitudes and behaviour can be seen as outcomes of value orientations. For instance, because I put a high value on equality, I have a positive attitude towards Negroes and behave accordingly towards them. At the same time my actual attitude and behaviour can be evaluated and measured against the standard set by my value. Although some writers have treated values as an adjunct to studies on attitudes, it seems to us that they deserve more detailed consideration.

Finally we intend to discuss behaviour change in relation to values and attitudes. A considerable amount of research has been done, especially on attitude change, which does not link the values and attitudes to behaviour. There is an intrinsic interest in understanding what factors can induce someone to change his attitudes, and we shall be concerned with some of these studies later. But the link between values, attitudes and behaviour should not be disregarded. The reason should seem obvious. Most psychologists take the view that a concept such as attitude is best viewed as an 'intervening' or 'mediating' variable. By this is meant that we have to posit a construct which we assume to exist, but which is not directly observable. We can observe someone voting on a number of occasions for a particular politician. We explain his regular behaviour in responding to stimuli (elections, candidates) by saying that this person has a positive attitude to the candidate or his party. The attitude is thus inferred from regularities of behaviour in the presence of specific stimuli, and ultimately must be tied to those observable phenomena.

It appears that underlying some studies of attitude change has been the assumption of a causal link between attitudes and behaviour, and the belief that by changing a man's attitude one could hope to change his future behaviour. These assumptions may be wrong. Cohen (1964) pointed out 'Thus attitudes are always seen to be a precursor to behavior, a determinant of what behaviors the individual will actually go about doing in his daily affairs ... Until a good deal more experimental investigation demonstrates that attitude change has implications for subsequent behavior, we cannot be certain . . . that the attitude concept has any critical significance whatever for psychology.' This need to look at attitude–behaviour relationships is echoed by Festinger (1964) whose theory on attitude change has led to much research in this area. Abelson (1972) also questions the causal link between attitudes and behaviour in a contribution titled 'Are attitudes necessary?' We shall therefore bear in mind the question of whether there is a relationship between values, attitudes and behaviour. We shall also be asking which of the three is the best agent for a change in the other two. We may find circumstances in which values and attitudes change as a function of a behaviour change.

The assumed tie-up between attitudes and behaviour can also be noticed if one considers real-life situations in which a person or group of people attempt to change someone's attitude. Although they seem to share the assumption of many psychologists on the importance of attitudes, their ultimate focus is on behaviour. The advertiser attempts to change preferences (attitudes) towards his own brand in order that people should *buy* his product. The politician talks and writes with the view of influencing you to *vote* for him. The parent and teacher reason with the child to make him *work* or *behave* better. The social worker or psychiatrist reasons about or explains the client's attitude to himself and others in the hope that as a result of this, the person will *function* better. These examples highlight both the importance of the concepts under discussion, and also the pervasiveness of our belief in the importance of attitudes.

The orientation of this book is psychological. What does this imply? It implies that our starting point of enquiry is concerned with the needs and aspirations of man and his attempts to fulfil them; that is why we asked earlier, why we need attitudes and values. But these concepts are not the exclusive province of psychologists, they can also be of interest to sociologists. Sociologists, however, would be asking different kinds of questions. They could ask, for example, which cultures give rise to different kinds of values and attitudes, and why? One may substitute for the word 'cultures', nations, political parties, professional roles or family structures – the approach would still be the same. That is, the focus is on some kind of organization, and the individual is ultimately seen as combining within himself the influences and constraints of these organizations of which he is a part. This is of course an oversimplification of the sociological approach, but it will serve to highlight the main difference between this and the psychological one mentioned above. The psychologist may also be interested in, and take note of, social factors in relation to values and attitudes; but his point of departure is still the individual. In the last resort, if attitudes are acquired by every man, they must serve some basic function for the individual. Kelvin (1969) deals with this question in detail. 'Man can only cope with his environment if that environment is reasonably orderly and predictable, so that the individual, and the group or society, may know where they stand and what to do.' He further argues that the main way in which we make and keep our social environment orderly, and predictable is through values, by which some things are good, others bad, some better others worse. And 'Attitudes are, in fact the fundamental processes or systems whereby the individual orders his environment and behaviour on the basis of values'. If values are the measure by which we order our social environment and attitudes are the manifestations of this order, it links these clearly to the basic assumption of man's need for order and certainty. A moment's reflection should convince us that this makes sense.

To be able to organize one's diverse thoughts, preferences and actions into a coherent pattern reduces uncertainty and allows one to operate without the stress of continuously having to evaluate all the stimuli in order to respond correctly. In a sense therefore we have categorized or prepackaged certain stimuli to certain responses. However, equally important is the fact that this imposing of some order on the social universe makes it easier for others to interact with us; further, because we are enabled to understand other people's 'package' we can interact, and thus understand them. This need for categorization and order, and by extension the need for other people to validate our order, is possibly one of the most important assumptions of social psychologists. Our certainty of the correctness of this order, in our values, attitudes and behaviour, is probably crucial to the way we evaluate ourselves. But categorization and order lead to complete predictability. In making this a central need of man we ignore the notion of 'choice'. Some research by Zimbardo (1969) and others seems to show that man has the need to feel, and to be seen to be free to choose and act and thus not be completely predictable. Kelvin is aware of this point and claims that *because* man has choice to act in a variety of ways his world would appear chaotic (unpredictable) without the imposition of some order. It appears that against the backcloth of order man still needs to experience himself as a free agent. We *react to* an ordered environment, but we also want to *act on* the environment.

In this introductory chapter, we have attempted to spell out the orientation of this book and especially to look at some of the assumptions which underly the research done in relation to the concepts of values and attitudes.

2
The nature of values

In this chapter we will take a closer look at the way *values* can be defined. We shall then discuss why it is important to study this concept in its own right although it is clearly related to that of *attitudes* (see D4). This will be followed by a demonstration of how values can be measured, with particular reference to one approach which suggests a psychological method of changing a person's values.

Psychologists are notorious for their obsession with definition. Yet to the extent that definitions can help us to describe their functions and see how they are related to our concepts, they are important. It is also interesting to notice how a researcher's particular definition of a concept arises from, and also determines, the kind of investigation he is undertaking. It is even more essential to be clear on what we mean by values because it is often used synonymously with attitudes.

It is worth emphasizing from the start that psychologists use the terms 'values' and 'attitudes' mainly in connection with the study of man. Psychologists will however differ on the degree of importance we attach to the term 'values' – for some it may be no more than a figure of speech; for others it is of central importance.

The most extreme position is probably held by B. F. Skinner (see A3, B1, F8). The title of his recent book, *Beyond Freedom and Dignity* (1971), contains two words denoting values. Nevertheless, any attempt to understand the power that values, or attitudes, may exert on man in regulating or changing his behaviour, is to Skinner a non-issue. This is not the place to discuss Skinner's work in detail. What is important to us here is that Skinner does not conceive of any qualitative differences between animal and man, and thinks, furthermore, that the only relevant data for their study are directly observable phenomena. These are environmental stimuli and responses. He is mainly concerned with probabilities – whether a certain kind of behaviour will be repeated or not – and this depends greatly on the kind of reinforcement this behaviour received previously. As he puts it 'behaviour is shaped and maintained by its consequences'. When Skinner refers to these psychologists who think that beliefs or needs or opinions are supposed to change when we change our mind, he asserts that 'What is changed in each case is the probability of action'.

In Chapter 1 we pointed out that the concept of 'values' cannot be observed directly, and also said that it is considered useful for the study of man. Neither of these two points fits into Skinner's approach. His outlook is based on the two general propositions of determinism and behaviourism. Determinism in its extreme form will encompass *all* kinds of behaviour, whether we talk of the predictability of a young child's behaviour, or about the person who feels that he was 'driven' to an action, or about ourselves in our daily interactions. Behaviourism, with its focus on directly observable phenomena, will include all forms of human thoughts and aspirations, as these too are meant to be contingent on reinforcement principles. Determinism implies in our context that for a person to say 'I choose Joan' (rather than Jean, as a friend) is meaningless. It follows from behaviourism that mentalistic concepts like freedom or values are not worth studying since nobody can directly observe them. Skinner will concede at most that behaviour which will be repeated because of its positive consequences will be labelled by man as having value. We have spent some time in outlining Skinner's approach although he 'devalues' the concepts that we are interested in, because he represents, in an extreme form, a very influential school of thought, which is by no means dead. It is extreme compared to others only in its 'all or none' approach. Values are more clearly defined by Jones and Gerard (1967): 'Any singular state or object for which the individual strives or approaches, extols, embraces, voluntarily consumes, incurs expense to acquire is a positive value ... Values animate the person, they move him around his environment because they define its attractive and repelling sections.' For Jones and Gerard 'a value expresses a relationship between a person's emotional feelings and particular cognitive categories'. 'War (cognitive category) is bad (expression of emotional feeling)', thus becomes a negative value. 'Food is good' is a positive value. Since any cognition can have an emotion attached to it, the number of values a man can have is only constrained by the number of cognitions he can hold. This definition is extremely wide since it will include objects as well as states of mind and will not distinguish in its definition between the value of diamonds or religion. But because of its vagueness it can allow for the possibility that these subjective evaluations can be acquired in different ways and have differing degrees of centrality for a person.

A different emphasis is made by Allport (1963). He writes: 'A value is a belief upon which a man acts by preference'. This general statement must be seen in the context in which he continues: 'We know a person best if we know what kind of future he is bringing about – and his molding of the future rests primarily on his personal values'. It is evident that this approach is in sharpest contrast to that of Skinner. It acknowledges choice in man and moves the concept of values to the centre of life and its aspirations. One can also presume that this accords more with our traditional definitions.

The most important attempt in recent years to come to grips with the question of values is that of Rokeach (1973). We shall therefore explain his approach in greater detail. His main definition is: 'A value is an enduring belief that a specific mode of conduct or end-state of existence is personally or socially preferable to an opposite or converse mode of conduct or end-state of existence'. If you substitute for the phrase 'mode of conduct' the words 'honest' or 'kind'; and for 'end state of existence' the concepts 'security' or 'salvation' – the definition becomes reasonably clear. Like Allport, and perhaps more explicitly so, Rokeach puts the emphasis on values that *people* have rather than on those that are said to inhere in *objects*. If you believe that to be honest is more important than to be self-controlled or that salvation is more important than pleasure, then honesty and salvation will have greater value for you. Note that Rokeach gives values something of an enduring quality. His definition allows for the emotional component of a value – that one feels good or bad about it. It also encompasses a motivational component, the striving towards their attainment. The affective and cognitive components are implied in his definition by the word 'preferable'.

In the quotation of Rokeach's definition of values, we mentioned 'mode of conduct or end-state of existence'. These terms refer to what he labels *instrumental* and *terminal* values. He points out that there are divisions within these terms. Instrumental values can refer either to morality or competence. An example of the former would be to behave honestly, of the latter to behave logically. Within the category of terminal values he points out that some are in their focus intrapersonal (peace of mind), while others are more interpersonal (brotherhood). Most theorists have ascribed prescriptive and proscriptive attributes to values, that is, they have argued that there is an 'oughtness' about them. Rokeach, however, points out that the degree and extent of this will be partly a function of society's demands with regards to the value. The value 'salvation' is more likely to be shared and to be insisted on in a Catholic than in a secular state. Others, especially the moral instrumental values (e.g. honest, loving) are more likely to have a universally agreed attribute of 'oughtness'.

Rokeach identifies two important functions which values serve. One such function is as *standards* which will guide our conduct; they help us, for instance, 'to evaluate and judge, to heap praise and fix blame on ourselves and others'. A second function which he calls *motivational*, is concerned with the component which expresses our striving towards its attainment. We strive to be honest etc. In this sense, striving for their fulfilment represents to him a human need. If values occupy a central role in our lives, then this need to achieve standards of excellence becomes conceptually tied to our need to maintain and enhance self-esteem. If I value honesty highly, then my *attempts* and *achievements* to be honest must affect my self-evaluation. To the extent that others share my values and are aware of my honest behaviour, my self-esteem will be enhanced by their reactions. One can also understand the perceived discomfort of a lowering of self-esteem when one has violated one's achieved standards (guilt) and is seen by others to have done so (shame). It will remain to be seen whether the orientations of Allport and Rokeach, which imply that man can act and not only react, are more acceptable than behaviourism. They also claim that concepts like values and attitudes are of central importance to the study of man – this too will have to be shown to be the case.

Values and attitudes compared

One distinction between these two concepts which is frequently made is, that values occupy a more central position than do attitudes. Consider some of your values and observe how your attitude towards a person or object can arise from them. You value honesty highly – you have a negative attitude towards a person who consistently tells lies. Or you value justice and you have a favourable attitude towards the politician who in your view may help to bring it about. Katz and Stotland (1959) made such a distinction between values and attitudes. Value systems are, in their view, not concerned with specific objects or persons, while attitudes are. Attitudes to a group of people can be associated with two or more values. A positive attitude to Jews is more likely to be associated with people who value equality and freedom highly. On the other hand a number of attitudes can be associated with one value. Consider a person who puts a high value on a world at peace – one can think of a number of attitudes that would cluster round this central value. Looked at like this, values are more abstract than attitudes. One would also assume, if one agrees with this distinction, that values are more central in that they are more deeply enclosed in the person, perhaps part of his personality structure. If this is so then it should be more difficult to change a man's values than his attitudes.

Perhaps because values are less specific than attitudes, one can not so easily detect them in behaviour patterns. We tend to behave favourably or unfavourably towards those people or things about which we have attitudes; but the same does not apply to values.

There is an additional reason why a distinction between the two concepts is worth making. If one holds certain values, one does not hold them a little or much, but completely. This is particularly the case with moral values. We do not for instance believe in little or more freedom or honesty, we believe and strive for its complete realization. What we allow for are two things. We can say that if we have to choose we may value security more highly than freedom, should an issue arise where these two values appear to clash. Another possibility is that a person may be in a conflict situation because two equally important values appear to clash on a particular issue. The reason for this total belief in values may be because we conceive them as standards of behaviour, and therefore, although we may not be able to attain them fully, they do not allow for 'half measures'. We suggest that this is not quite the case with attitudes. One can speak of degrees of positive or negative attitudes. This distinction between values and attitudes means that the two may require different kinds of tools to measure their strengths or importance for a particular person.

The measurement of values

Allport, Vernon and Lindzey (1951) developed a standardized scale to measure the relative importance individuals attach to six value orientations (see D4). These are

(1) Theoretical (truth) (2) Economic (usefulness)
(3) Esthetic (harmony) (4) Social (altruistic love)
(5) Political (power) (6) Religious (unity)

The authors devised statements which give expression to the above value orientations. In a forced-choice pencil and paper test, people scored their preference for a particular statement as it was put in opposition to *one* another, or a *number* of statements. From an analysis of all the responses, the authors presented a profile or 'psychograph' for each person. They claim high reliability for this test. (Reliability of a test is the measure of its stability; that it is an *accurate* score.) They also claim validity for this measure of values, in that it distinguishes between people along their dimensions. They showed clergymen had relatively high religious and social values while students of business administration rated highly economic and practical values. This has been the most widely used test of values.

The limitations of this measure of values are clearly set out by Allport (1963). In the first instance the six value areas are rather restricted. We could think of values not touched by their test, like pleasure or security. The values chosen seem to cover an idealized version of socially acceptable values. Perhaps they best describe the aspirations of a middle class student in the 1950s. Secondly, the test deals with relative preferences but does not tap the strength of conviction behind these preferences. Two men may put a similarly high value on power in comparison with other values, but do they necessarily agree on the strength of the drive – to what extent will each pursue the realization of this value? The Allport, Vernon and Lindzey test can not deal with that type of question. According to Allport the test has been most useful for counselling purposes as it can indicate what kind of subject particular students ought to study at college, or what kind of career they ought to take up.

In spite of these limitations of the test, we will mention one study, quoted by Hollander (1971), in which the value test was used to make predictions in an experimental situation, This example will at the same time illustrate the importance that people attach to value systems, as suggested by Allport. Vaughan and Mangan (1963) gave subjects the Allport–Vernon–Lindzey value scale, isolating two value areas for each individual subject. On one of these the subject had a high, on the other a low score. On the basis of this information the authors designed a modified Asch group conformity experiment (see B1, B2). In a series of experiments dealing with perceptual tasks Asch (1956) placed a naive subject next to a number of strangers who had been briefed to respond as instructed by the experimenter. The perceptual task was to call out which of three vertical lines flashed on a screen was equal in length to a standard line placed a little distance from the three variable lines, e.g.

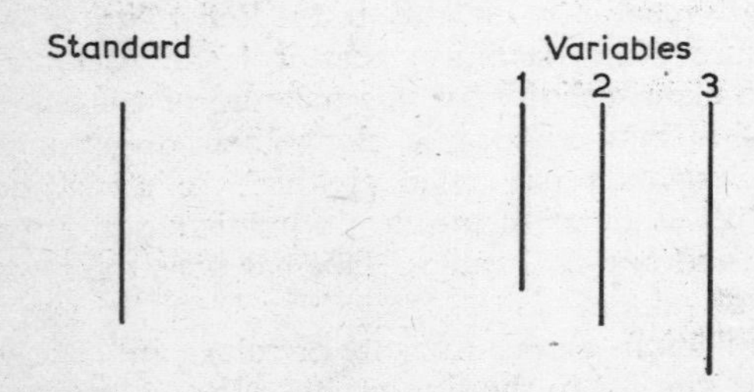

On certain critical trials the stooges were instructed to call out the wrong answer, i.e. No. 3. Assume the naive subject is the last of the group asked to call out his answer, will he conform to the group's opinion or will he maintain his own and say correctly, No. 2? Asch usually found that about one third of the subjects would conform with the majority opinion. Vaughan and Mangan used Asch's procedure, but instead of vertical lines they projected statements onto the screen. These statements pertained to the naive subject's low and high value orientation instead of vertical lines. Here is an example:

(1) Production efficiency is a matter of vital / minor* concern

(2) Theology must be considered a fruitful / fruitless* study

(the words with an asterisk are the misreadings of the stooges). The prediction of the authors was that the subjects would conform more in low value areas than in high. This was borne out by the results. A subject who valued highly the orientation embedded in sentence (1) but not sentence (2) would far more likely conform in (2) and read 'fruitless' instead of 'fruitful'. They argue that resistance to group pressure where it runs counter to one's perception is highest when a value of great importance to the individual is at stake.

Rokeach's value measure

In his revised measure of values, Rokeach (1967) uses two lists of words or short phrases.

List A contains eighteen terminal and List B eighteen instrumental values.

List A

A comfortable life
An exciting life
A sense of accomplishment
Family security
Freedom
Happiness
Inner harmony
Mature love
National security
A world at peace
A world of beauty
Equality
Pleasure
Salvation
Self-respect
Social recognition
True friendship
Wisdom

List B

Ambitious
Broadminded
Capable
Cheerful
Imaginative
Independent
Intellectual
Logical

Clean	Loving
Courageous	Obedient
Forgiving	Polite
Helpful	Responsible
Honest	Self-controlled

The respondent is asked to arrange each list by ranking the values in the order of their importance to himself. Any difference in people's values will show up by the difference of ranks they assign to the same thirty-six values.

How reliable is this as a measure of an enduring value system? A test-retest after an interval of approximately fifteen months yielded the relatively high reliabilities of .69 for terminal and .61 for instrumental values. If the retests are taken after shorter time-intervals the reliabilities are even higher.

Rokeach claims that values are closely related to attitudes, and that they will distinguish between people of different political orientations and commitments.

Let us illustrate his attempts to demonstrate that this is so by the following studies, which will also show the methodology he uses for his classifications. He postulates that four political orientations of: Communism, Socialism, Capitalism and Fascism are related to two value dimensions. These are Freedom and Equality. Following this conceptualization he arranged the four ideologies in the following way along the two *independent* dimensions.

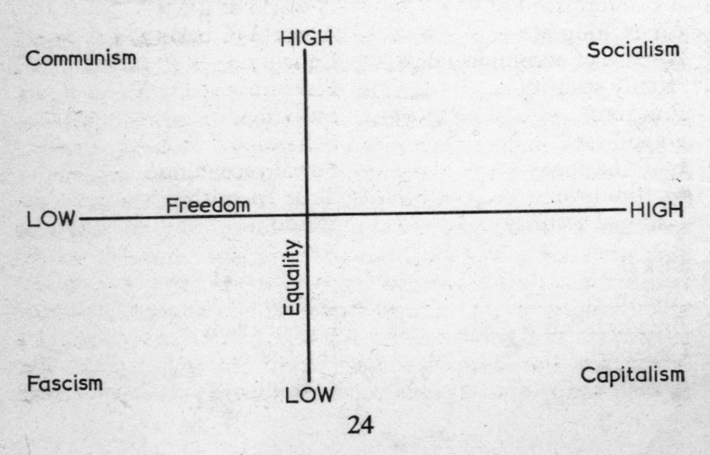

Thus Communism = Equality high, Freedom low
Fascism = Equality low, Freedom low
Capitalism = Equality low, Freedom high
Socialism = Equality high, Freedom high

To validate this two-dimensional model, Rokeach made a content analysis of written material which represented the four ideologies. This material was taken from the writings of Lenin (Communism), Hitler (Fascism), Barry Goldwater (Capitalism) and from contributions to a symposium on Socialist Humanism. Two judges rated 2000-word passages from each of the four categories to establish reliability of scoring. This was followed by the main study in which one judge using 25,000 word samples, counted the number of times each of the terminal and instrumental values was mentioned. The final count for each value is the number of positive minus the number of negative statements about that value. On the basis of this he established a rank order of terminal values for each set of writings. He found that the four differed on a number of values but those showing the greatest differences were Equality and Freedom. This is illustrated in the table:

Rank position out of seventeen terminal values

	Socialists	Hitler	Goldwater	Lenin
Equality	2	17	16	1
Freedom	1	16	1	17

(The greater the number the lower the rank)

He claims that his finding supports his two-dimensional model and the importance he attaches to his measure of values.

The distinction between the four political ideologies refers to systems of political thinking rather than to specific political attitudes. In another investigation however, Rokeach used an American sample of voters who had declared their preference for one of seven presidential candidates. He compared respondent's presidential choices with their own rank orders of Rokeach's value measure. The seven groups ranked Freedom equally high, the average placing is 3. There was a very noticeable variation on the value of Equality. For example Kennedy supporters ranked it fourth, Nixon's twelfth and Wallace's fourteenth. For Rokeach this finding confirms his model, but in the context of that presidential election the choices were on the Socialist–Captialist dimension. The Communist–Fascist (i.e. Freedom) issue was not in question.

We shall quote one additional finding by Rokeach because it attempts to extract from a ranking procedure differences in *commitment* to specific political ideologies. His reasoning is as follows: If Freedom and Equality are the fundamental parameters of political orientations, his measure should be able to differentiate between an active and inactive supporter of the *same* party. The activists should value or disvalue one or both of the critical items *more* than the non-activists. From the above quoted sample on presidential candidates, Rokeach could distinguish between activists and non-activists. Comparing their results on value ranking, he found a tendency for activists to give more extreme ratings on a *relevant* value. Thus Wallace-non-activists rated equality fourteenth and freedom third, activists rated them eighteenth and first respectively. This shows, therefore, that activists of a political attitude orientation have more polarized (extreme) value rankings, wherever these are related to the issue.

How shall we evaluate this test and its use in the above examples? Rokeach uses two lists with a total of thirty-six values. Hs assumes, mainly on intuitive grounds, that this number is about right. Although Rokeach has gone to some length to decide which values to include in the lists, and they are more numerous than those of Allport *et al*, he admits that other people could have included other values. A respondent can still only rank what is given in the test; he cannot go beyond it. This is one limitation of Rokeach's test. Another limitation is that ranks give no indication of the degree of importance one attaches to a value except in relation to another value. Two people can rank Equality first out of eighteen values. This in itself does not tell us whether their intensity of feeling and commitment, to their first choice, is the same. To be fair to Rokeach, the study we quoted on within party differences between activists and non-activists attempts to extract qualitative differences from differential rankings.

Rokeach claims that his measure 'is sensitive to differences betwen cultures, institutions, group membership and personal experience'. These are claims for the measure's usefulness and its validity. Any test which can distinguish between people in a meaningful way when extensive knowledge of their past personal experience would yield similar results, has a good case for its validity. In the studies quoted here Rokeach has shown that certain values are related to specific attitudes. These are descriptive findings of a correlational nature (see A8). They can not show that a person is a fascist *because* he rates Equality and Freedom low in his scale of values. Nor do they show that people change their values because they have become fascists. Rokeach does believe however that values determine attitudes and subsequent behaviour. His attempt to prove a causal relationship between these goes well beyond the scope of this chapter.

3
The nature of attitudes

In the previous chapter we came across the term attitudes on a number of occasions, mainly to contrast them with values. We will now focus more precisely on ways the term *attitude* has been conceptualized and defined. We shall then outline a number of techniques designed to measure attitudes.

In contrast to values, the study of attitudes occupies a dominant role within social psychology. McGuire (1968) pointed out that some theorists in 1920s regarded attitudes as so central a concept for the field that they equated social psychology with the study of attitudes. The interest in this topic has not waned; annually many books are published on some aspect of this area.

When it comes to definitions of attitudes, although almost every author coins his own, we will not concentrate on their differences. We shall approach them via a more general orientation and then note some of the special emphases. If you have a positive attitude, say, to your parents, this is viewed by psychologists as a mental readiness to feel, think and be inclined to behave towards them in a positive manner. They maintain that each attitude has an affective, cognitive and conative component. In the example given it would imply that not only do you feel positively towards, you also have bits of positive knowledge about them, e.g. they are honest and kind. Any action which you undertake towards your parents is not part of the attitude itself; only the *tendency* to act (e.g. to approach, kiss, help, etc) is part of the attitude. If attitudes, like values, refer to phenomena which cannot be directly observed but only inferred, the action itself cannot be a component of the attitude concept. These general features are said to hold for all attitudes, whether they are towards individuals (your parents, or a friend) or group of people (Russians, Americans). What we have said seems to fit the more formal definition given by Krech, Crutchfield and Ballachey (1962) '... attitudes are enduring systems of positive or negative evaluations, emotional feelings, and pro or con action techniques with respect to social objects'. We mentioned earlier that the concept is seen as a pre-disposition or mental readiness which implies that people have this tendency, or motivation, to view the social world within defined categories of goodness and badness. This aspect comes out clearer in the following definitions. 'Attitudes are predispositions to respond, but are distinguished from other such states of readiness in that they predispose toward an evaluative response' (Osgood, Suci and Tannenbaum, 1957). Or '... an attitude is a predisposition to experience, to be motivated by, and to act toward, a class of objects in a predictable manner' (Smith, Bruner and White, 1956). From these definitions one can get an overall picture of the way to conceptualize attitudes, despite different emphases which authors place on details. You will, for instance, have noticed how Osgood *et al* stress the affective, while Smith *et al* put greater emphasis on the motivational-cognitive factors. If every attitude consists of the affective cognitive and conative component, one would expect a high correlation between the three components. This means that a high positive rating on the affective dimension should be matched with a similar one on each of the other two components, and *vice versa.* Such correlations are reported by McGuire (1968). He quotes a study by A. Campbell *et al* (1960) in which they found a correlation of .80 between the cognitive components of political attitudes (self-ratings on political issues) and the conative component (actual voting preferences). Similar high correlations are reported by Vidulich and Krevanick (1966) between cognitive and affective components of an attitude towards Negroes.

Another approach to the study of attitudes which manifests consistency between its components is one by Rosenberg (1960). Assume we have affective and cognitive ratings of someone's attitude; if we change just one component, what will happen to the other – will it fall in line with the changed component? This is the problem Rosenberg attempted to solve experimentally. Such an experiment is, however, difficult to set up. When we say we have changed someone's affect for negroes and watch what effect this has on his cognition about negroes, it is very likely that in our attempts to change his affect, we *at the same time* tend to inform him of new cognitions. Rosenberg used posthypnotic suggestion to get a pure measure of the effect of changing one attitude component only. Using easily hypnotized subjects he divided them, on the basis of a pre-experiment test, into those with pro- and anti-Negro attitudes. During hypnosis the opposite feeling was suggested to them, e.g. 'on awakening you will feel very positive towards negroes and like them'. On a following attitude test it was shown that the cognitive component had adjusted itself to be in line with the new feeling, irrespective of whether the change was directed towards the positive or negative position. There were only eleven subjects in this experiment, and it is just possible that good hypnotic subjects differ from the general population in other respects than their suggestibility. Otherwise this seems a good demonstration of the need for consistency between the attitude components.

Attitude measures

Attitudes, not being directly observable, can only be measured indirectly. As we shall see, most of the measures concentrate largely on measuring one or other of the attitude components mentioned earlier. We need a measure in order to compare individuals or groups, and also to record changes within the individual when he has changed his attitude. Ideally, a test that is both reliable and valid should also be sensitive enough to discriminate between both fine and gross differences along the whole dimension. Only a small difference on an attitude scale may distinguish the extreme from the very extreme anti-Semite. But that difference may be the critical factor in deciding whether the person will behave violently to Jews or not. Because we need fine discriminating points most of the tests rely on verbal reports.

The range of verbal response measures that one could use is very wide. At one extreme one can visualize questions which on the surface have nothing to do with the attitude in question, and to which the responses, too, are open-ended. At the other extreme, and this is the most frequent way of measuring attitudes, there are standardized statements which clearly refer to the attitude; the subject's response is clearly defined and minimal in his personal expression, since he merely ticks the statement with which he agrees. We hope to illustrate the different techniques and their respective advantages. We assume of course that subjective dispositions when expressed verbally can be expressed as a numerical value. Another assumption is that questions designed by the experimenter have the same meaning for all respondents.

Thurstone scale

One of the first techniques was developed by Thurstone in 1929. Given any attitude object, Thurstone believed that one could construct a series of statements which ranged from the extremely unfavourable to the extremely favourable. These statements express positions along the whole scale which have equal intervals between them, as the one-inch difference between two and three inches is the same length as that between three and four inches (see A8). The objective nature of this measure, should enable one to distinguish between people as to the *degree* to which they differ on an issue. How can one construct a test to satisfy Thurstone's objectives? He took an issue like 'attitudes to church' and assembled a set of 130 statements from a variety of sources, representing both favourable and unfavourable dimensions. These statements were given to a large number of judges with the request to arrange all the statements into eleven categories, labelled A–K, the midpoint F representing the neutral position. The judges were asked *not* to express their own attitude to the statements but to indicate solely the degree to which the statement is an indication of favourableness or unfavourableness on the issue of 'church'. From these 130 statements, Thurstone selected about 20 which constituted the final scale. The criteria for their selection were that their ratings had the highest agreement between the judges and their scale value contributed to a total scale of approximately equal intervals between them. Each statement had a numerical value which was the averaged score of all the judges' ratings. The subject was then presented with a randomized presentation of the twenty statements and asked to indicate those with which he agreed. By checking the numerical values attached to the 'ticked' statements the experimenter was able to obtain a measure of the subject's attitude.

Here is a selection from such a group of statements – used, in this case, to measure attitudes to killing.

0.5 To take the life of another human being, whatever the reason, is the same as murder.
1.0 It is difficult to foresee circumstances in which one is entitled to sentence someone to death.
4.0 In times of war one may have to execute traitors, in order to save the lives of others.
7.0 The death penalty ought to be restored in the case of murdered policemen.
9.0 The abolition of the death penalty has led to increases in all kinds of violence.
10.0 If a person kills someone else it is only fair that he should suffer the same fate.

It is possible now to imagine twenty such statements, and that an individual can have a score based on the total value of the statements with which he has agreed. We will discuss the Thurstone scale further when we compare it with other measures. What must already have become clear is that the construction of the scale is very time-consuming. The same effort must be expended on every attitude to be measured, whether the number of respondents is 10 or 1000.

Likert scale

A different test, which has become very popular, was designed by Likert (1932). If one of the statements on his scale were to read:

> 'The abolition of the death penalty has led to increases in all kinds of violence'

you would be asked to indicate which of the five ratings you agreed with:

(1) strongly agree (2) agree (3) undecided (4) disagree (5) strongly disagree

The number in front of the responses represents the weights attached to them. Instead of the weighting being done by the experimenter as with Thurstone's scale, here the subject chooses his own degree of agreement to which a numerical value is assigned. The total score of the subject is the sum of the values which he has attached to all the items on that issue. Likert, too, started the construction of his scale with many items relating to an issue. A pool of judges was then required to indicate their *own* attitudes by responding to all the items on the five-point scale. The main criterion for including an item in the final test was its internal consistency. If the score on an item discriminates between those judges whose total score was high and those whose score was low, the greater the consistency between a person's score on that item and all the other items. This is a much simpler test than Thurstone's and it's reliability is claimed to be at least as high. Because of the way it is constructed most of the items on the Likert scale will fall at the two ends of the scale and have less discriminative power as we move nearer to the neutral point. The two tests discussed so far consist of statements which also deal with the cognitive component; the next is rather different.

Osgood's Semantic Differential

The above technique, named after its senior author, was published in 1957 by Osgood, Suci and Tannenbaum. Their original research was concerned with the measurement of meaning that people attach to words. With reference to concepts, like attitudes, the technique is to present subjects with a set of semantic scales based on bi-polar adjectives. A shortened example could be:

FATHER

	+3	+2	+1	Neutral	−1	−2	−3	
good	—	—	—	—	—	—	—	bad
beautiful	—	—	—	—	—	—	—	ugly
strong	—	—	—	—	—	—	—	weak
active	—	—	—	—	—	—	—	passive

Osgood uses a minimum of nine bi-polar adjectives, and subjects are asked to indicate with an X their own position on the scale. In our example we have used a seven-point rating scale with the midpoint standing for neutral, or 'don't know'. Numerical values can either go from +3 to −3 or in some cases 1–7 with number 4 as the midpoint. The individual's score is his total score on all scales for that concept. Osgood *et al* have found that the meaning of a concept has three main factors: the evaluative (e.g. good–bad); potency (e.g. strong–weak) and activity (e.g. active–passive). The most important of the three factors is the evaluative one, accounting for over 70 per cent of the variance. This factor is closest to the affective component of an attitude. This scale is easy to design, the adjective is usually chosen on intuitive grounds as being relevant to that dimension. As Osgood uses single word constructs, rather than statements, it is not surprising that his measure strongly emphasizes the emotional factor which we attach to an attitude object. In this he differs from the preceding tests, and also from the following one.

Social Distance Scale

In 1925 Bogardus designed an attitude scale, known as the Social Distance scale. This test, and those derived from it, comes nearest to measure the conative, or tendency to act, component of an attitude. His original concern was to design a measure of the degree of acceptance or rejection by natives of foreign nationals. He used seven statements denoting different degrees of intimacy and respondents had to indicate which of these was acceptable to him, when referring to specific nationals. The classifications include: (1) To close kinship by marriage; (2) To my club as personal chums; to (6) As visitors only, in my country; (7) Would exclude from my country. With this test one can measure differences between individuals towards the same group as well as within-person differences towards different groups. Triandis (1971), for instance, has made extensive use of this technique. By varying factors like religion and race, and looking at this cross-culturally he sought to find those independent variables which contribute most to a person's social distance score.

Gespi (1945) modified the technique to give a measure of a person's attitude to conscientious objectors.

The test is a very useful and relatively simple tool, but its main limitation appears to be that it is a test of 'acceptance' of stimuli that are usually perceived negatively, e.g. foreigners.

Sociometry

Another measure in which the stimulus object is undefined and left to the respondent is that of sociometry (Moreno,

1953). One can use any natural group, be it a school class, members of a club, or a work organization. Everyone is asked to name his most preferred partner for a specific activity and then to rank the rest of the group in order of preference. Typical questions may be 'Who would you most like to sit next to?' or 'go on holiday with?'. Within any group one can get a picture of the 'overchosen' person, and the opposite, whom nobody chooses as a partner for that activity. While this test concentrates on preferences with regards to behavioural intentions, one can get additional information by asking a further open question: 'Who would you most want to sit next to *and why*?' This can give us some knowledge about the affective and cognitive components of the respondent's attitude. This test has not been used extensively in attitude research. We have however mentioned it because special circumstances may force the researcher to use and adapt the most appropriate tests available. This is well illustrated by the approach of Pushkin (1967). He looked at a sample of three- to seven-year-old children to study their ethnic choices through play situations. These were to be related to mothers' attitudes, but also to the kind of contact the children had with 'foreigners'. He used three tests, which owe something to both Bogardus and Moreno. For the first two tests, he used 'black' with 'white' dolls. In the 'tea party' test the respondent, represented by a white doll, was the hostess and 'sat' at the top of the table in a doll's house. There were ten dolls (black and white) and the child was asked to place them on chairs around the table. There was only room for five chairs, who would be left out? This allows for a measure of preference *and* rejection. The second, a see-saw test, had the respondent again presented as a doll. The child had to choose from the mixed dolls, the order in which he would want to be partnered on the see-saw. In the third, the 'houses test', the child is shown pictures of families, some with English features, others with Negro, Indian and Italian. Faced with a picture of a row of houses, the child is told to imagine that the one in the centre is his/her house, and asked to put the family pictures against those houses near their own according to their preference. It seems to us important that these tests can be quantified and are tapping different dimensions – playing outside, inviting to one's home, and living in close contact with. Do these three tests show a unitary factor which may be termed an attitude with behavioural intentions? Pushkin found that results on the three tests were significantly related to each other, that is, a child with a very negative attitude to Negroes would score highly on all the tests.

The tests which we have reviewed require respondents to make choice between alternatives. The latitude of responding is circumscribed by the set questions of the researcher. They have the advantage that scoring of the results is easy because the responses are unambiguous. The drawback of such methods are the following:

(a) When we are dealing with socially non-desirable attitudes, subjects' responses may be coloured by the need to not appear to be 'deviant'. This has been recognized in personality studies, and some provision has been made for it. For instance the Taylor Manifest Anxiety Scale (Taylor, 1953) required respondents to answer 'true', 'false' or 'don't know' to many questions designed to measure their chronic anxiety. It also incorporates a number of 'lie questions' which try to establish whether the respondent is answering sincerely, or in accordance with how he would like to appear to others. Attitude scales, in general do not allow for this. The more 'sensitive' the topic in question, the greater the possibility of invalid responses.

(b) Attitude measures are, as the name applies, *measures* and nothing else. They do not tell us *why* a person holds a certain attitude, and what makes it salient to him. Such knowledge, however, could be valuable to those who are interested in attitude maintenance and change. It is as if one had a thermometer which measures body heat without telling us why the temperature rises, or how we can lower it. The approach of attitude researchers has therefore been to vary experimentally one of the factors which is not derived from the information given by the respondent on his attitude scale. A more dynamic approach of assessing a person's attitudes is usually found among students of 'personality' and clinicians (see D3 and F3).

(c) If we give a repeated attitude measure before and after intervention, to what extent is the score on the second measure influenced by subjects' replies on the first measure? Having committed themselves in the first instance it may affect a person's second response in a variety of ways.

(d) Some people would argue that we may not be aware of some of our attitudes. Psychodynamic psychologists would certainly argue that some attitudes, especially those involving conflict or ambivalence, may in part be unconscious (see D1, D3). However honest the respondent's replies to the attitude questions, they would not represent his 'real' attitudes. What are the alternatives? One could have an extended interview, in which the questions would be probed in depth. Or one could employ more disguised techniques, by which subjects are questioned on issues which are only subtly and not directly related to the object in question. In the former instance, the interview, people will differ on the *interpretation* and *scoring* of the material produced during the interview. Independent judges would have to be used who agreed on these points. Pushkin (see above) used this technique for mother's attitudes to ethnic minorities. Nor could we legitimately compare responses across different interviews. There are bound to be differences between interviewers in the way questions are asked and the manner in which respondents' answers are reinforced by the interviewer. These can have important effects on the results obtained.

An example of a disguised measure is the *projective* technique. Best known from clinical and motivation studies, this involves the presentation of ambiguous stimuli on which the subject 'projects' his attitudes. Imagine being presented with an untitled picture of a white girl sitting at a table and a coloured man entering the room. The 'meaning' of the picture is kept to the minimum, there is little furnishing of the room and the facial expression of the two people is not made manifest. You are asked to look at the picture for about twenty seconds and then given five minutes to write a story about the picture. It is presented as a test of creative imagination, and it is emphasized that there are no right or wrong answers. The story about the picture should answer four questions: (1) What is happening? Who are the people in the picture? (2) What has happened to them in the past? (3) What are their thoughts and wants? (4) What will happen next? One would have to devise a scoring system to account for the number of positive and negative elements in the person's 'story' about the boy and girl. Although the person is asked to imagine what is going on in the picture, the assumption is that subjects will project their own attitudes onto the picture, and that this will even tap his 'unconscious' attitudes *because* he is not aware of revealing himself. The technique is similar to the interview in that neutral judges have to agree on the scoring of the responses. It does, however, largely overcome the question of experimenter effect discussed earlier.

We have discussed a range of techniques for measuring attitudes. Which one is used in a particular study often depends on the kind of question one is interested in answering. It is however also influenced by the need to get quick results from many subjects, and some types of tests lend themselves more easily to this. Ideally one would want that the same subjects be given several tests, which overall could yield information about the components of the attitude in question and tell us something about its relationship to other facets of the person's mental make-up.

4
The determinants of values and attitudes

In the previous chapters we have discussed the nature of both values and attitudes and their relationship. Given that every individual holds such concepts within his cognitive framework, it now seems apposite to try and understand just how they are acquired.

The acquisition process is complicated and remains a matter of theoretical controversy. We are interested in both the general mechanism which transmits the values and in the more specific. It can be seen that there are at least four levels or stages in which this problem can be viewed, although they are at no time mutually exclusive. Thus one can look at the *personality* of the individual alone and the predispositions he brings to bear on any situation (see D3). One can further look at the *interaction* of the child and adult with other members of his social milieu – the process of *socialization* (see C3). The next, and more molar level, is that of *group* membership and how this affects attitudes and values both within the individual and in relation to others not in the group (see B2, B4). On the next level one can analyse the attitudes and values which are transmitted to the individual as a member of a *social class* (see B5).

Obviously, although this may seem a neat classification, one must beware of oversimplification. It is thus necessary to be aware that, for instance, unless one takes a purely genetic view of personality (which is untenable), socialization processes are a major factor in personality, personality a major factor in many group memberships and so on. An attempt will be made to discuss the levels separately, but reference to and interrelations among them can hardly be avoided if the discussion is to be plausible. Here we are not so interested in attitude and value *change*, although they are obviously of relevance, as these will be discussed more formally in later chapters. Rather we are looking at the mechanisms by which values and attitudes are *initially transmitted* and how they are modified by and modify later interactions.

Personality

Firstly, it seems appropriate to look at basic personality factors which are the predisposing characteristics governing *which* attitudes and values will be assimilated by the individual throughout his life.

Initially, let us consider Eysenck's personality theory (see D3, D4). Eysenck does lay quite a strong emphasis on the genetic basis of behaviour. He proposes a physiological theory concerning individual differences and the extent to which socialization processes are accepted. He is mainly concerned with the dimension of introversion and extraversion and its physiological correlates. Extraverts need more external stimulation than introverts. What then does this mean when considering acceptance and determinants of values and attitudes?

Eysenck assumes, within a neobehavioural framework, that the transmission of social values is determined by conditioning mechanisms (see A3). Introverts are more susceptible to conditioning; extraverts, on the other hand, are more difficult to condition, and thus tend to internalize the attitudes and values of society less readily – they tend to be 'undersocialized'. Eysenck validates this by citing a study in which a high correlation was found between childhood extraversion and recidivism. So what is it that Eysenck is saying? Based on a physiological and genetically inherited make-up, one can be classified as an extravert or an introvert. Because of one's physiology one is more or less susceptible to conditioning and thus more or less likely to become socialized with the appropriate values and attitudes of society. This is a trait which each individual brings to bear on any attempt made by society to control his behaviour, thoughts and feelings.

A second approach to personality in this context is the famous conceptualization of the 'Authoritarian Personality' (see D4). Rather than talking in terms of innate structures, the authors (Adorno, Frenkel-Brunswik, Levinson and Sanford, 1950) are conceptualizing a type of person, and the correlations and covariants likely to be found within this person's attitudinal system. The study originally began with the study of anti-Semitism in Nazi Germany and allowed an analysis of ideological content, measurements and associated personality characteristics. The elaboration of the theory in 1950 provides a meticulous methodological and conceptual examination of the area, and no attempt will be made here to cover all the arguments; rather, only the basic levels will be examined.

The authors contend that anti-Semitism is part of a general factor rather than an isolated prejudice, in that those individuals who make negative attitudinal statements about Jews also make them about Negroes and other minority groups. They also found a coherent cluster of statements regarding authoritarian attitudes, particularly deference to superiors, hostility towards inferiors, unwillingness to introspect into one's feelings, and the inclination to project unacceptable impulses onto others. Using interviews and projective tests (see p. 37), they were able to investigate the world view of the authoritarian person and the attitudes about his childhood and family environment (for example, highly authoritarian individuals tended to have harsh and threatening home disciplines and retain a latent hostility towards their parents).

This conception was formalized in the widely used F-scale (Fascism scale), which measured prejudice indirectly without mentioning specific minority groups, and also illuminated underlying personality predispositions towards a fascist outlook on life. Thus, once again, we have a personality disposition which will operate during the transmission of values and attitudes; the extent to which these values and attitudes are accepted by the individual, and some intimation of how such an outlook is acquired, are also provided by the theory.

The next personality-type theorist to be considered is Rokeach (1960). He is convinced that the F-scale measures right-wing authoritarianism rather than authoritarianism in general. He believes that the only way to have an unbiased approach is to look at the *structure* of belief systems and not the content. He postulates a continuum between open and closed belief systems and suggests that the individual's responses are defined by his positioning on this continuum. Thus, an individual can believe in very left wing, permissive ideas but still espouse them in a closed or dogmatic way. Any given personality is seen as 'an organization of beliefs or expectancies having some definable and measurable structure', and the extent to which this individual's set of beliefs is open or closed is a generalized state of mind; this reveals itself in the way the individual accepts and rejects certain categories. There are three types of acceptance or rejection – those of ideas, people and authority (the latter is the authoritarianism factor involving prejudice and intolerance) and all three relate to the belief system.

So what actually defines an open or closed belief system? Rokeach has defined it as the extent to which an individual can receive, evaluate and act on relevant information received without being influenced by irrelevant factors arising from either within himself or outside. Such irrelevant factors are seen to include the reward contingencies present, the anxiety reduction possible, and so on.

Rokeach developed a scale to measure the ability, or lack of ability, to discriminate substantive information from information about the source and to assess the two independently. This was the Dogmatism scale, which also measured authoritarianism and intolerance. Further, he also developed an Opinionation Scale which measured general intolerance.

Thus the open/closed dimension within any individual's belief system will determine to a large extent, not the specific values and attitudes that the individual will hold, but the *way* in which he holds and espouses them. It also gives an idea of how resistant that individual will be to changing these values. We also have some hypotheses about how an individual acquires an open or closed system. People with closed systems tend to have high anxiety, and the closed system is assumed to represent a cognitive network of defences against anxiety often originated in childhood experience.

The final personality theorist we shall discuss crosses the boundary between personality *per se* and socialization. For Freud (see C1, D3), the acquisition of both morality and values and attitudes was embodied in the development of the superego within the child's personality through a process of *identification*, and this identification is initially with the parents. His theory also extends to the nature of the child's sexual identity which we will discuss in greater detail later.

By identification, Freud means the internalization of values of the models (the parents). Thus the superego, which includes the conscience and the ideal self, is formed at the resolution of the Oedipus complex. The Oedipus complex is assumed to occur in all boys (the feminine equivalent is the Electra complex). Briefly, it can be described as follows. The boy loves his mother and sees his father as a rival; because of his growing fear of castration he represses his love and desire for his mother and hatred for his father and accepts his father as a model for identification. When formed, the superego is a substructure of the ego. It is a guilt-producing and punitive structure that ensures that gratification of the *id* (the generic term for energies inherent in the system) is achieved in ways which are acceptable to society. Thus the conscience component suppresses instincts not acceptable to the ego-ideal.

The ego-ideal is seen as the perfected idealization of how one should be. This is formed through identifications in which the child, through an attempt to restore his own depleted self-love, incorporates his images of loved persons into himself. A series of such identifications leaves a sediment in the form of values and goals.

In this way, the child originally shares the values and attitudes of his parents, which are later replaced by those of the peer groups with which he identifies. In suggesting this idea, Freud comes closer to recognizing the role of society, in the form of the parents, as determinants of values and attitudes than do the former theorists. His, however, is a dynamic developmental approach which does not involve more abstract conceptualizations of the mature adult bringing certain cognitive and affective styles into the situation (as in strict personality theories).

So what other mechanisms operate in the socialization of the individual, and how do these lead to the transmission by society of values and attitudes? Obviously, one area in which socialization affects many of our attitudes is in the way that children attain a concept of their sex-role, and we shall later discuss this as an example of all the more general mechanisms purporting to operate.

Broadly speaking, socialization can be seen as the process whereby individuals attain the role expectancies, values and attitudes of society through interpersonal relationships. This process is not confined to the child but continues throughout adult life, for example when an individual occupies a new position or joins a new group. Socialization takes many forms and several approaches have been put forward to account for the way in which each individual, as a member of society, comes to acquire the relevant attitudes. As we have seen, some of the determinants may come from the effects of personality dispositions on the reception of the socializing influences. Nonetheless, both the child and the adult have to learn which attitudes and values are appropriate to his or her environment. One central approach to this question comes from learning theory (see A3, B1). It will be emphasized again and again in the following chapters how learning theory concepts are utilized to explain the parameters and conditions of attitude formation and change. Both classical and instrumental conditioning are seen as relevant within the socialization process. By *classical conditioning* we mean the process in which a stimulus (conditioned stimulus) is repeatedly presented at the same time or shortly before some unconditioned stimulus, and comes to acquire the power of evoking the response which initially could only be evoked by that unconditioned stimulus. *Instrumental conditioning*, on the other hand, consists of rewarding and/or punishing some acts and not others, thereby 'shaping up' behaviour in certain directions. Obviously, the most direct influences of a child's behaviour are the parents, and it is initially the parents, acting as societal agents, who are assumed to control the necessary environmental events which shape the child's behaviour (and thus, implicitly, attitudes until verbal statements of the child's attitudes are available). Thus they are able, through control of primary, and later secondary, reinforcement, to develop within the child values and attitudes that are consistent with those that they hold. (Secondary reinforcement occurs in situations where a neutral stimulus is paired with a primary reinforcer (e.g. food) and thus comes to produce the same effects upon behaviour as the primary reinforcer.) Once certain aspects of behaviour have gained value through this process of instrumental conditioning, neutral objects and events then acquire value by being associated with positively or negatively evaluated objects and events through classical conditioning. Thus a whole attitudinal network is set up, and this kind of approach allows specification of which attitudes are formed towards which objects and whether the attitudes are positive or negative.

As the parents' place is taken over by peer groups as being the most significant people in the individual's environment, this conditioning process continues to modify old attitudes and create new ones. Of course, as the child gets older, external reinforcement is no longer necessary as the child will reinforce himself when his behaviour or new attitude is congruent with the already existing attitudinal network.

Learning theory thus provides a coherent picture of some aspects of socialization and is obviously an appealing one. However, there are some aspects of the process which it cannot incorporate very elegantly within its formal structure. That children imitate adults is a well observed phenomenon. What is interesting is that they often enact the imitated behaviour at some later time when the model is no longer present. Attitudes and values can be learnt in this way, and it is a process quite distinct from the direct shaping procedures discussed above. Although most of the studies concerning imitation and socialization have concentrated on the behavioural reproductions by children of the models, imitation *per se* has been defined as 'the tendency for a person to reproduce actions, attitudes or emotional responses exhibited by real-life or symbolized models' (Bandura and Walters, 1963), which are assumed to be displayed through the behavioural phenomenon. Bandura (1969) contends that imitation is acquired both through *stimulus contiguity* (S-S learning) *and symbolic mediation* (via language and imagery). It is thus an active process with a number of variables operating (including motivation, reinforcement, attention and memory) in conjunction with sensory stimulation to determine the resultant performance. Bandura then extends this argument to an assumption of a generalization process. This is seen as a higher order form of modelling, where the child is able to abstract the attributes and rules of such behaviour. Once abstraction has taken place, these rules can be seen as a basis for acting in a particular way to a particular object, person or situation. That is to say, it becomes part of the attitudinal network. The extrapolation from behaviour to attitudes and values may appear a little tenuous initially. However, in a later chapter (Ch. 7) some very convincing evidence for just such a relationship is presented.

As mentioned before, one of the most obvious consequences of socialization can be seen in the adoption of specific sex-roles. For Freud, this comes about through identification as a result of conflicts. Freud assumes that every child is constitutionally bisexual, and the extent to which parent identification occurs will depend on the relative strengths of the male and female components. Usually there is identification with both parents, 'the relative strength and success of these identifications "determining" the fate of the boy's attachments and his character, his antagonisms and degree of masculinity and femininity later in life' (Hall, 1956).

Specific behaviour and attitude patterns are often attained through imitation as well. One often sees a child nursing a doll in the way the mother nurses a younger sibling, and then one hears the girl reprimanding and praising her doll after the manner of her mother. Likewise the young boy imitates the farmer's actions and tries to aspire to adult male standards (e.g. by saying 'I'm not going to cry, men don't cry'). All these things build up into an attitude and value system related to the sex-roles.

Adults, too, play a large part in this development; they strictly censure certain behaviours not appropriate to the sex of the child. Thus a boy who likes dolls is reprimanded for being a 'cissy' – and 'boys don't do that' is often heard. It is interesting to note that the female sex roles are not always regarded as so important; the female has hitherto been dependent on the male, which necessitates a much more well-defined role for the male. Thus for a girl to be called a 'tomboy' is less censuring than for a boy to be called a 'cissy'.

Education processes have for a long time maintained these roles; the girls studying arts, domestic science and needlework, the boys studying sciences, woodwork and engineering. More recently these definitions have been breaking down; although resistance remains, both in the attitudes of others and in the socialized attitudes and values of the individuals, the attitudes, values and role expectations of the two sexes are getting increasingly diffuse. One is obviously not suggesting that there are no genetic and physiological differences, merely that the attitudes and values associated with the sex roles are moving from a male–female distinction to one tailored to the individual's needs irrespective of sex.

Group membership
On the more molar level, we can now look at the effect group membership has on our attitudes and values and at the pressure which exists to persuade us to conform to norms. We will not deal specifically with prejudice (although this is obviously a relevant topic), as this will be the concern of the following chapter.

Every group which one joins, for whatever reason, holds certain social norms. A social norm is an expectation shared by the group members which specifies appropriate behaviour, thoughts, feelings and attitudes. Thus if one joins a Church of England Youth group one is expected to go to church, believe in God, and positively evaluate certain moral standards. Within any group there is a large amount of pressure on the new member, and existing members, to conform to this norm, and certain rewards and punishments are proferred to maintain it. In a group like a political system, certain explicit sanctions in terms of laws and enforcing agents exist. However, in smaller groups, these norms are often implicit, and the 'deviant' member only learns them when sanctions are called into operation. The communication of norms, or 'norm sending', is operated through three components of the group: (a) defining the attitudes and behaviour in question; (b) monitoring the extent of conformity; and (c) applying the relevant sanctions (Secord and Backman, 1974). However, the extent to which negative sanctions are applied and the amount of pressure exerted is limited to the extent of the cohesiveness of the group (Festinger, Schachter and Back, 1950).

In this way a group and the individual's membership of that group can act both to define, modify and maintain each individual's attitudes and values. Little modification is necessary if the individual voluntarily enters the group because he identifies with it, but great pressure to change can occur if the individual merely complies with the group for his own purposes, or if it is coincidental that he enters the group e.g. an individual taking a new job which, coincidentally, necessitates joining the office social club.

Sherif *et al* (1951, 1953, 1961, 1966) has made many studies of how the genesis of groups occur and how they react to other groups. Most of the work in this area has concentrated on intergroup hostility, conflict and prejudice. Sherif, however, studied children on camp sites and he described the status delineations, group products and norms, control over deviant behaviour and so on. He and his co-workers 'set the scene' for producing intergroup hostility, and showed how this conflict produced greater solidarity and positive attitudes within the group. He was ultimately interested however, in how, once group membership had determined the values and attitudes of the individuals towards the group and towards the out-group, one could then resolve the conflict by changing these self-same evaluations.

The study is detailed and long and a summary of his findings will be presented. Sherif maintains that when conditions involve goals, which are compelling for both the groups, and yet unattainable by one group independently through its own efforts and resourcefulness, cooperation will occur. If a series of such superordinate goals are presented, there is a cumulative effect which results in reducing social distance and hostile attitudes, and also leads to re-evaluation of the group and its members.

We have this far attempted to understand the effects group membership has on our attitudes and values, plus the effects of such membership on the attitudes towards other groups. Necessarily the process is somewhat more complex than that set out here and readers are directed to Secord and Backman (1974) for a fuller exposition.

We now move on to briefly discuss the relationship between certain attitudes and class membership. We shall consider, then, the part membership of a socio-economic class plays in determining our attitudes and values. Obviously the influence is strong, in that if the class we belong to defines the individual's environment to some extent, then the values transmitted through the socialization processes described above must be congruent with the class structure. The issue in question is whether certain classes have certain attitudes as distinct from other classes. Eysenck (1947) originally became interested in this topic and in the fact that although working class members are traditionally assumed to be more 'left wing', yet opinion polls found them to be more ethnocentric and less permissive in respect of, for instance, the death penalty, treatment of conscientious objectors, and sexual morals, than the middle class (Eysenck, 1970).

By statistically analysing a sample of questions concerning social issues, Eysenck has extrapolated two main factors which are orthogonal (totally independent of each other) that characterize the responses to these social issues. The factors are the R factor (which is the radicalism–conservatism dimension, and is assumed to be a general social attitude factor) and the T factor (the toughmindedness–tendermindedness dimension).

When equated for voting patterns, the working class sample was found to be more conservative and toughminded than the middle class, irrespective of whether they voted Liberal, Conservative, Labour or Communist.

This study provides an excellent end to the chapter, in that the themes initially picked up have been revisited. Eysenck projected his T factor onto the field already mentioned of introversion (tenderminded) and extraversion (toughminded). He suggests that specific patterns of social attitudes relate to specific social classes but *also* relate to personality factors. Eysenck avers that these two factors appear in the 'authoritarian personality' as a toughminded conservatism, and in the 'humanitarian' as a tenderminded radicalism. Maybe Rokeach's classification could be subsumed under these two factors too – there is really little evidence to assume that any one of the presented continua is more correct or useful than others.

We have thus come a full circle. We have looked at some aspects of personality, socialization mechanisms and influences, group and class membership, and we have returned to personality in an attempt to discuss what could affect the values and attitudes we hold. We have also tried to keep in mind that there are two-way relations and interactions between each level under discussion, i.e. personality affects socialization which in turn affects group membership. *But* the converse is also true.

5
Prejudice

Most of this book is devoted to general attitudes and ways of changing them. The topic of prejudice falls within the attitude domain, and can be said to be an example of an extreme attitude. To be prejudiced against Negroes implies, as with any other negative attitude, that one is predisposed to feel, think and behave towards them in a predictable negative way. To discriminate against Negroes is the actual behaviour arising from the prejudice. While prejudice is therefore a part of our general theme, we feel that it deserves a short chapter of its own.

What makes the topic special? In the first instance prejudice is a historical phenomenon, it has been with us for a very long time, and is still with us. It is also very pervasive; we speak of prejudice against women, religious groups, social minorities and almost any other group one can think of.

Secondly, there have been times when the intensity of prejudice and discrimination was so great that it was held to justify and lead to the lynching of Negroes, the killing of Jews or Vietnamese civilians.

Thirdly one tends to feel helpless when attempting to change a person with a strong prejudice. Most efforts at changing such attitudes and behaviour seem pitiful in their ineffectiveness. In the early 1930s German Jews wore their war medals of the first world war; they published endless material to show what good Germans they were, and had been for hundreds of years. In retrospect we know how ineffective these attempts were at reducing prejudice, but we also feel that this racial prejudice has an immovable quality against which any attempt to change it looks desperate and naive.

Finally, prejudice is something we see in others and accuse them of it. We rarely admit it of ourselves. Aronson (1972) recalls, how he was made aware of a mild prejudice in himself. He had quoted an experiment by Janis and Field (1959), which appeared to show that women are more easily persuaded than men. A female psychologist pointed out to him that this generalized conclusion about women was unwarranted. The topics under discussion, in the experiment, dealt with issues that were probably of more interest to men and about which they had more knowledge than women. The *right* conclusion would have been that people are more easily persuaded on topics about which they know and care little.

In theory one can be prejudiced *for* someone or a group as well as *against* someone. One can thus imagine a continuum of prejudice from extremely favourable to extremely unfavourable. In practice however it is mainly used with a negative connotation. The range of such prejudices is very wide and goes beyond that of discrimination of minority groups. It includes for example problems in rural India of introducing new farm machinery, or general acceptance of contraception for women. There are also examples of a dominant minority showing strong prejudices against the majority group, as is the case in South Africa.

We can approach the problem by looking at possible *causes* of prejudice, and their *maintenance*. You will recall that in Chapter 1 we emphasized the need of human beings to categorize the environment and to predict outcomes with minimal cues. One way of doing this is through the perceptual cognitive process of stereotyping. We assign certain characteristics to a particular group; on meeting any of its members, we expect him to be a typical member of that group and to share all its attributes. This fulfils an important function in our daily life. But while it has similarities with prejudice, it appears to us to be different in most important aspects. Stereotyping is basically neutral. It can refer to a mixture of positive or negative characteristics or features which have no evaluative content. My stereotyped view of Italians may be that they are dark, musical, lazy and fun-loving. Prejudice on the other hand has predominantly an evaluative core. Furthermore my stereotyped view of Italians is easily disconfirmed on meeting some Italians that are not lazy. With prejudice however, disconfirming evidence will be explained away as being atypical of that person; or that this person is atypical of the group to which he belongs. An anti-Semite will not be swayed in his views of Jews by evidence of their charitable behaviour, nor the Negro-hater by seeing intelligent, efficient Negroes.

We will also come across the theory of social judgement in Chapter 6. We shall see that holding extreme views which are important to the self-image causes one to perceive discrepant views as being more opposed to one's own than they are in reality. This approach seems to be of greater value to an understanding of prejudice and its resistance to change. Can we relate prejudice to perception of the self? Does it enhance one's self-concept, and therefore become personally important. There are a number of psychological approaches to prejudice that may have a bearing on this question. In the previous chapter we came across Adorno's notion of the Authoritarian Personality and Rokeach's of Dogmatism. Both refer to specific personality characteristics that could predispose people to be prejudiced.

During their intensive clinical interviews, Adorno and his associates uncovered a number of factors which they related to prejudice. What clearly emerged is that the prejudiced person is basically insecure. He bolsters his self-image by perceiving the world in sharp contrasts of 'black and white'. At the cognitive level he sees himself as good and belonging to the 'white' category. He cannot tolerate ambivalence about himself and others, which makes him conform to his own group and be aggressive to outgroups. In this view prejudice is linked to the perception of the self, and because it is tied to personality characteristics the target of the prejudice could be any outgroup.

Another approach to an understanding of prejudice is less tied to personality factors and concentrates more on present life experience. It is known as the *scapegoat theory*. The basic proposition is that frustration leads to aggression – when the legitimate target of the aggression cannot be attacked it will be diverted on to targets where it is condoned or even encouraged. This will lead to temporary relief of tension, and will externalize the blame which could have been directed against the self. Using out terminology, frustration can be viewed as an experienced helplessness in face of a desired goal. It is a threat to one's self-image, primarily because the non-attainment of the goal could also reflect on the person's inability to achieve it.

There are a number of studies in which frustration was experimentally manipulated and scapegoating observed (Berkowitz, 1961; Miller and Bugelski, 1948). One experiment is particularly relevant to our view. Weatherley (1961) gave an anti-Semitism scale to subjects on the basis of which he divided them into those high and low on the scale. Half the subjects were subjected to very insulting remarks while filling in a questionnaire. They were then given picture story-tests – with the request to tell a story about each picture. Some pictures depicted people with Jewish-sounding names. An analysis of the data showed that subjects 'high' on anti-Semitism directed more aggressive acts towards the 'Jewish' pictures than those low on anti-Semitism. But this difference in aggression was *confined* to the 'Jewish' characters and not the neutral ones. This finding is important because the experimenter manipulated frustration by insulting individuals who could do little about it; it lowered their self-esteem. It also shows that the aggression is not 'blind' but requires a target that is already disliked. Since disliked groups already 'have faults' in the eyes of the beholder, one can shift blame and aggression onto them. To eradicate them may appear as the ultimate attempt to forestall any 'future threats'.

We have argued that threat to one's self-esteem may be an important factor in overt prejudice. It should therefore not surprise us that people whose social status is low or *declining* are more likely to be prejudiced than those whose status is high or *rising*. In our competitive system, in which we give high value placings to earnings and status, this is to be expected. Low status and income are not critical, however, provided they are rising, since at a psychological level rising earnings and status can enhance confidence in the self.

The scapegoat theory seems limited in its explanatory value. It is difficult to see any frustration or aggression directly related to a peasant woman being prejudiced against contraception. The South African white may show aggression to the black – where is the frustration? What they may have in common is a perceived threat to the self. The peasant woman may see her own value and self respect as a woman and wife that bears children. Contraception may threaten this. The white South African can only justify his behaviour of economic and personal discrimination, without damaging his self-evaluation, by devaluing the blacks, and holding on to the belief that they are barely human.

We must not, however, overstress purely psychological explanations. They may account for the latent predispositions and causes of prejudice. In reality the prejudiced *person* flourishes as a member of a prejudiced *group*. Membership of his own group constrains him from directing his prejudice towards it, but at the same time allows him to direct it to any outgroup. He can therefore operate within the norms of his society. Pettigrew (1958) believes that conformity to the dominant group norms is a critical factor in prejudice. He showed that antiblack prejudice in the United States and South Africa was related to the measures of *general conformity* to group norms and not to scores on the F-scale, which measure personality dispositions. For these people the need to conform and not to deviate from the group was paramount. The risk of being different is too great. It seems to us that conformity may be an explanation for the *cause* of milder prejudices. When it comes to active discrimination and the ill-treatment of minorities, conformity is best seen as favouring the *maintenance* of an existing prejudice. It also *legitimizes* extreme behaviour based on prejudice.

We have tried to understand the powerful hold that prejudice has over people by pointing to the need to externalize blame and contempt when one's self is threatened. What is difficult to explain is the excess of the behavioural reaction, as, for example, lynching. At the dynamic level it points to something more deeply pathological. At the cognitive level it may be noteworthy that manner of speech and propaganda have supplied us with justifications for extreme behaviour patterns. We kill animals, for our safety, our food and pleasure. Despised minorities are frequently categorized as being like animals. 'They breed like animals', 'they behave like beasts' etc. By making a qualitative distinction between ourselves and the despised group, we sanction and justify their treatment as animals.

If one could assume that prejudice results from lack of knowledge of what the real attributes of the minority group are, the problem would be relatively easy. We would present prejudiced people with the right information in the most persuasive manner. We know that this is wishful thinking since we are not dealing with a mild, irrelevant attitude.

Because prejudice has mostly been studied as a group phenomenon, and not in a clinical setting, research has focused on diminishing those factors which maintain and legitimize prejudice. These attempts can be looked at as a means of removing the present reinforcers of prejudiced behaviour. Alternatively, they can be seen as ways of changing the perception of the minority as an out-group by incorporating them into the main-group.

One approach to the reduction of prejudice has been to increase contact between members of the two groups. As has been discussed in B2, studies on inter-personal attraction show that opportunity to interact with another is associated with increases in mutual liking. To repeat a famous sentence of Homans', 'You can get to like some pretty queer customers if you go around with them long enough'. Will mixed housing estates and integrated schools reduce prejudice against minorities? As people interact and know each other more, it ought to increase the degree to which they see themselves as similar. Secord and Backman (1974), after reviewing the literature on this topic, come to the following conclusion. Increased interaction reduces prejudice, because the minority group person disconfirms an expectation about him. But if I work next to someone and find out, for example, that he is not lazy as I had expected, my change towards him is only in his *role as a worker*. Generalizations to other situations are minimal.

What seems to have a greater effect is interdependence of behaviour, because in this situation both sides share a common fate. The unifying factor which reduces general prejudice seems to be the common attempt, by cooperation, to overcome an external obstacle or enemy. This has been shown in field studies (Star, Williams and Stouffer, 1958) with soldiers who had fought together during the war. It can also be seen from the study by Sherif *et al* (1961) quoted in the previous chapter. The hostility between the two groups was mainly reduced by creating situations, which made it necessary for both to cooperate in removing frustrating obstacles. In these situations reinforcement has become dependent on unity rather than division.

We began this chapter by stressing that prejudice is an extreme *attitude* which can lead to extreme forms of behaviour. We end it with the thought that communal *behaviour* may diminish prejudice. What is the psychological nature of the reward which people experience as they jointly overcome an external force? These themes are the recurring topics of this book.

6
The importance of communication factors for effective attitude change

Let us conceive of attitude change as a problem of effective information communication flow between two people: A the persuader and B the person to be persuaded. We can then envisage a number of problem areas that need investigation. As Lasswell (1948) put it, we must ask, '*who* says *what* to *whom* and with what *effect*?' Using different terminology, one can investigate the effectiveness of the persuasion as a function of differences in (a) the source of the message (b) the message itself and (c) the type of receiver (audience) of the message.

This approach, which is associated with the Hovland–Yale school, systematically changes the independent variables of the communication process to measure their effect (dependent variable) on attitude change. McGuire (1969) considers that an additional classification may be useful. The dependent variable of 'attitude change' he suggests, is too vague. We should also ask ourselves to what extent has the target person:

(a) *attended* to the message,
(b) *comprehended* the message,
(c) *yielded* to it,
(d) *retained* the message,
(e) *acted* as a result of this message.

By focusing on these five processes we may be able to distinguish what kind of manipulations lead to greater effectiveness. To give one example, different results on yielding to new information may be due to one group having comprehended it better because they are more intelligent.

This approach, mainly initiated by Hovland, is a pragmatic one. Firstly it looks at experimental variables without having generated some overall theory which postulates some dynamic process in the target person. Secondly, it arose from and is concerned with pragmatic questions. An example of this was the problem posed to Hovland near the end of the second world war. After victory in Europe there was an understandable apprehension in the US government about the morale of the American troops who were required to continue fighting in the Far East. What would be the best propaganda (information) to influence the soldiers' attitude to continue to wage war? (You will note other questions of a similar applied nature in our later discussion.) Hovland and his associates sought to bring such problems into a laboratory situation in order to be able to isolate the relevant variables.

Source effects

A classic experiment designed to investigate the effect of type of source or agent in attitude change was reported by Hovland and Weiss (1951). What effect has the credibility of the *source* (the persuader) on subsequent yielding to his message? Hovland and Weiss gave student subjects an opinion questionnaire which included questions on the critical topics which were the object of the experiment. One week later the same subjects were presented with four 'newspaper articles'. Each article dealt with one of the critical issues, in some cases presenting arguments in favour and in others arguments against the issue. In addition, for some subjects an arcticle would be presented as coming from a credible source, e.g. issue – drugs: source – medical journal. Or coming from a low credibility source, issue – drugs: source – a mass circulation paper. After reading these articles, they answered a second questionnaire, from which present attitudes could be extracted. Comparing the pre- and post-test for attitude change in direction of the message, they found that for high credibility source the change was 22.5 per cent but for the low credibility source only 8.4 per cent. This is a statistically significant difference and must be attributed to the different source manipulation. How do we know that credibility of the source was a meaningful variable for the subjects? Do they think that a medical journal is more trustworthy on the issue of drugs than a mass circulation paper? Hovland and Weiss had data from the first questionnaire in which the subjects had to rate different sources for trustworthiness. The results showed clearly that subjects agreed with the experimenters' assumptions of the relative trustworthiness of these sources. We can thus identify 'credibility' as an important source variable for effective attitude change communication.

Recalling McGuire's five factors mentioned earlier, we could ask (a) whether the importance of high credibility source is related to the *attention* that subjects pay to the message and (b) whether the observed different results last or whether the credibility factor leads to a momentary difference only. Hovland and Weiss investigated both questions. With reference to (a) they found no difference in the amount of information retained (and thus attended to) between the two conditions. With reference to (b) they observed what is known as a 'sleeper-effect', i.e. after a lapse of time a person will be *more* persuaded by the content of the message and less influenced by the credibility (or non-credibility) of the source. Hovland and Weiss, upon giving their subjects a third questionnaire one month later found increasing acceptance of the 'low' source's message but decreasing acceptance of the 'high's'. With reference to this sleeper effect Kelman and Hovland (1953) found similar results to those mentioned. In their case the message was the advocacy of very lenient treatment toward juvenile delinquents, treating them as sick children. In three conditions the source was either introduced as a presiding judge of a juvenile court (positive), a member of the audience (neutral) or as someone with a shady past who had transgressed the law and was out on bail awaiting trial (negative). An additional questionnaire, given after three weeks, showed a marked decrease in the immediate impact of the 'judge' and an increase the persuasiveness of the 'rogue's' message. What we hope to have illustrated is that results from one experiment, however clearcut the evidence, often lead to further investigations of the factors involved. A positive result on source trustworthiness leads to questions of *why* it is more effective and also whether it will *always* be more effective?

We shall now consider some additional research which attempts to clarify the notion of credibility as an important factor in attitude change. In a study by Johnson and Scileppi (1969) it is shown that credibility is of importance only on attitude issues in which subjects have only a mild interest, but that when their ego involvement on an issue is high the effect vanishes. The reason for this may be that greater self involvement makes subjects pay more attention to the content of the message and less to the source. One can argue further that high involvement gives a person a greater investment in his own attitude which makes him more suspicious of any attempts to modify his position. An earlier study by Walster and Festinger (1962) may throw some light on this. They investigated the perceived intention of the communicator. In one condition subjects thought they had overheard the message, while in the second condition the message was directed to the audience in the usual manner. Walster and Festinger found the 'overheard' condition superior in changing people's attitudes – but only on issues in which subjects had a high personal involvement. Thus the 'overheard' message that husbands should spend more time at home was only more effective with married but not with single women. What is surprising, as the authors have already noted, is that this finding holds for the situation in which the communicator *supports* what the subjects want to believe. There is in fact some evidence (Brock and Becker, 1965) that an overheard communication is more effective than the usual communication with an 'involving topic *only* when the persuasion leads to a desired result, but not when it is involving and undesirable.

If a communication is overheard, the communicator can have no ulterior motive. If it is not overheard, but presented directly, then the communicator may be suspected of giving desirable information for his own ends. Mills and Jellison (1967) showed not only that agreement with a communicator's position is higher in the undesirable than in the desirable condition, but also that in the desirable condition the communicator was rated (by subjects) as being less sincere, less honest and more cynical. He was also considered to be more opportunist and more tactful but also less likeable. One other study will be quoted which highlights the importance of perceiving the communicator as honest and personally disinterested for more effective persuasion. Walster, Aronson and Abrahams (1966) report a study in which adolescent school children were given one of four prepared news interviews to read. The topic of discussion was the degree of power that prosecutors and police should have in Portugal. The content was varied between *for* more power and *against* more power for the prosecution. The source was also varied between low prestige (a criminal serving a prison sentence) and high prestige (a prosecutor who has sent more men to prison than any other prosecutor). In the condition in which the criminal argued for more power to the prosecutor (against self-interest) he effected more attitude change than the prosecutor (for self-interest). In the same vein the subjects rated the criminal in the above condition as being more honest and influential than the prosecutor. The important factor is not general credibility and expertness but the credibility of the person in the particular situation; the perceived selfishness of his motive appears crucial.

Message factors in attitude change

Confidence and uncertainty

The message, or argument, that people use in order to persuade someone to change his attitude is to some researchers the core of the problem to be investigated. After all when we investigate 'who' persuades 'whom' – the question arises 'with what?' How was the message put across? One interesting investigation concentrated on the degree of confidence expressed in the message via language and non-verbal factors. Maslow, Yoselson and London (1971) report two experiments that attempt to clarify whether the manner in which a message is delivered is a critical factor regarding attitude change. The basic design of the two experiments is similar, and is based on the jury system of our courts. Subjects are presented with written documentation of a law case to enable them to decide whether they consider the accused guilty or innocent. Before they decide they are also asked to study an argument in favour of the accused – similar to a counsel for the defence. It is this last mentioned 'argument' which the experimenters varied. Although the essential content of the message was identical in both conditions one group was presented with arguments put forward in a confident tone, e.g. prefacing statements with 'Obviously', 'I believe', 'I am quite sure', while the second group had the same arguments presented more tentatively with expressions such as 'I don't know', 'I'm not positive', 'I'm unsure' in the text. The number of subjects agreeing with the 'counsel of defence' was significantly higher where the message was put across in a confident verbal manner. In the second experiment a neutral sounding tape was prepared again as a plea for 'not guilty'. An actor, was asked to mouth the message alternately in a confident, neutral and doubtful manner. Following this exposure the number of subjects who were sure that the plea for the defence was correct was highest in the 'confident' condition, less so in the neutral and least of all in the doubtful one. Their point is that 'a source is increasingly persuasive as his message increases in confidence whether expressed over linguistic or kinesic channels'. As the authors themselves say, what needs careful analysis especially with reference to the second experiment, is to isolate which non-verbal cues transmit the confidence of a persuader. We know intuitively that confidence is an important factor, whether it be in the parent, educator or therapist, in effecting change in someone else's behaviour. What remains unclear is why this should be so. Nor are we, as yet, able to go much beyond labelling some performance as confident without understanding its components or limits.

Fear arousal and persuasion

One message variable which is of potential interest to people is whether a rational appeal is more effective than a more emotional one, or vice versa. Experimental data on this issue are not at all clear. Different results have been published, some of them contradictory. The main reason for this contradiction is probably the difficulty of agreeing on what is an emotional and what is a rational appeal. This has become clear in an experiment by Ruechelle (1958) who found that 'judges' could not agree on the classification of material which was intended to serve as a rational or emotional message.

This is probably one of the reasons why research has been restricted largely to examining the effects of fear arousal. In a typical experiment the degree of fear will be varied and this fear refers to potential dangers to the person if he does not change his attitude and behaviour. If fear is a drive, then its motivational strength should increase the greater the fear, and acceptance of any recommendation (attitude change) should be facilitated. One could also speculate whether intense fear may not lead to inattentiveness, or to people defending themselves by generating opposing arguments rather than accepting those of the persuader. The classical experiment on this issue was done by Janis and Feshbach (1953). The topic chosen was dental hygiene, which included specific recommendations on how and when it should be performed. What the experimenters varied between three groups was the degree of fear of what may happen if the recommendations are not taken up. In the strong fear appeal condition, relative to the moderate or mild condition there was much greater emphasis on pain from toothache, needing dental treatment which is also painful, and possible secondary diseases including blindness and cancer. A control group was also used which received a talk on a different topic. Janis and Feshbach found that there was a positive relationship between degree of fear appeal and degree of worry about teeth as a result of the communication. But on two indices: (a) reported changes in toothbrushing practices and (b) attending a dentist during the following week, only the minimal fear group 'conformed' significantly more than the control group. The high fear appeal group differed in no way from the control group which had no issue-relevant talk. The authors conclude that 'the evidence strongly suggests that as the amount of fear-arousing material is increased, conformity to recommended (protective) actions tends to decrease'. We shall see that later research has rejected the above conclusion. What needs pointing out is that the above approach is primarily concerned with behaviour change as the dependent variable. In fact part of the talk was concerned with a discussion of the proper type of toothbrush to be used. A questionnaire response showed that all the three experimental groups showed a significant change in accepting such conclusions compared with the control group. One may have to separate the effects of different kinds of communication and changes in one's beliefs about the object, intention to behave differently and actual behaviour change.

The most systematic research on the effects of fear appeals is that by Leventhal (1965). In contrast to Janis and Feshbach they found a positive relationship between degree of fear arousal and attitude change. In one experiment the topic was the seriousness of tetanus and the need for anti-tetanus injections. While greater fear arousal led to increases in the belief in the importance of having a tetanus shot and intention to have one, this in itself did not lead to the behavioural change in having an inoculation. For this to occur an additional factor was required. This the authors call the 'high availability' factor. In this condition subjects were also told that the University Health Service expressed the hope that all the students would avail themselves of the necessary action to protect themselves, and they were given a detailed plan of the location of the health service and its times of opening. Furthermore, they were told to look at their timetable and locate a time when they would be passing the centre to have the inoculation. Leventhal's approach implies that a fear arousing appeal leads to two distinct reactions: firstly, to dealing with the immediate fear, and secondly, to coping with the danger spelt out in the communication. He argues that some responses to fear, like avoidance of thinking of the danger or bringing up counter-arguments, could be detrimental to the 'desired' coping behaviour, i.e. having the inoculation. When specific recommendations for the coping behaviour are made, this will eliminate 'various inward-turning inhibiting features of the fear state'. A factor which may have played a significant part in the behaviour change of the 'high availability' group, is that of expectancy. In this condition the student-subjects were told, as we noted earlier, that the authorities wished them to have an inoculation, and they may have perceived this as a necessary part of being a 'good student'. What appears from studies on fear appeal is that greater fear leads to more attitude change. Translating this into new behaviour requires something more. Perhaps this is some commitment to, or engagement in the new behaviour, if only at the cognitive level: 'I ought (am expected) to have an inoculation; I will do so tomorrow at twelve noon, when I pass the Health Centre!'

One- or two-sided presentation of message

A consideration in presenting an argument is whether giving *both* sides will be more persuasive than giving one side only. A study by Hovland, Lumsdaine and Sheffield (1949), using mass propaganda to change soldiers' attitudes showed the following: Those soldiers who had finished high school education were more influenced by the two-sided, while those less educated more by the one-sided communication. Furthermore, those whose initial attitude was similar to that of the persuasive message were more effected by the one-sided argument; the opposite held for those whose initial attitude was against. One should notice that those findings do not deal with long term effects, nor with the persistence of beliefs in the face of counter propaganda. In applied settings such variables as the above may be crucial. Who has to be persuaded, and do I want to change his attitude or bolster his existing one to make it more effective for a change in behaviour?

Primacy or recency effects

There are many occasions on which people are exposed to two opposing arguments. Has the order in which they are presented any effect on the degree of persuasion? If the first message has the greater effect it is known as the primacy, if the second as the recency effect. On the one hand we know how powerful first impressions are in influencing our perception. On the other hand, the more recent messages should be better remembered as more distant events are more forgotten. An issue like this can have important practical consequences. Two political candidates follow each other on television; counsel for the prosecution always presents his case before the counsel for the defence. Hovland (1957) quotes a number of studies which contradict an earlier finding by Lund (1925), who had put forward the law of primacy in persuasion. In their own studies Hovland and his associates were able to isolate those factors which may favour either a primacy or recency effect. The first communication is likely to be more effective if both sides of the argument are presented by the same person and subjects are not initially aware that conflicting arguments will be put forward. An additional important factor favouring primacy is subjects' public commitment at the end of presenting the first message. In Lund's experimental set-up subjects filled in three attitude questionnaires, before the experiment, after the first message and at the end of the second message. One could argue, and this suggestion comes already from Lund, that subjects' commitment as expressed by the second questionnaire would tend to lessen the effects of the second message. Hovland and his associates found such a factor, favouring the primacy effect only when subjects were told that their opinion on the issues were going to be published in a magazine. In this case their public expression of opinion tended to make the first communication more salient. This was not the case when the opinion ratings were given anonymously. That the primacy effect is partially dependent on public commitment is understandable. Committing oneself in public has more of the quality of *behaviour* than a private commitment. The latter is more likely construed as a temporary cognitive position. We already know from the work by Brehm and Cohen (1962; see next chapter) that a behavioural act is a powerful reinforcer for the attitude to which it is related.

Explicit–implicit conclusions
Among other message factors which have been investigated is whether the persuader draws explicitly the conclusion of his message or whether he leaves this to the target person. As McGuire (1968) has pointed out, the original hypothesis, partly arising from non-directive therapists like Freud and Rogers (see F3), predicted greater attitude change in the non-explicit condition. However, experimental evidence, for instance Hovland and Mandel (1952), has shown the opposite to be true. McGuire comments that implicit conclusion drawing may be more effective if we are sure that the person has drawn the conclusion for himself. What may have happened in studies favouring explicitness, he suggests, is that subjects were either not motivated or not intelligent enough to draw the conclusions. Accordingly, McGuire argues one would expect the 'implicit' to catch up with the 'explicit' as subjects have more time to draw the right conclusions, and also that the 'explicit' technique should be more effective with less intelligent subjects. He quotes some evidence for both predictions. Perhaps a more interesting question is the persistence of the attitude change once it has taken place arising from either of the two conditions. One would predict that because of greater personal commitment in the 'implicit' condition, the subjects' involvement would make the initial attitude more enduring.

Receiver factors

When we considered source and message variables of the communication process we paid little attention to the person to whom the message was addressed. This factor, the receiver variable, could not be completely ignored, as mentioned earlier in this chapter on credibility and ego-involvement. We have just referred to receiver variables in our discussion of explicit conclusions and intelligence of the receiver. Our more systematic exploration will focus on two areas. The first will deal with variations in the initial attitude of the target person.

The second will deal with the possibility that some people are more easily persuaded than others irrespective of the topic of the persuasive communication.

Intraperson factors. Let us assume that we want to measure someone's attitudes on two topics. We use the Osgood Semantic Differential scale (see p. 33). The scale's range is from −3 (very negative) to +3 (very positive). The subject rates both topics positively: one is assigned +3 and the other +1. You advocate via communication a negative position which rates as −2. Is the probability that you can induce any attitude change the same for both topics? Or has a more extremely held attitude less chance of being altered? Assuming you can shift his attitude on both topics, would the *degree* of movement be the same? Another question worth asking is: What kind of attitude is the target person expected to change? He may give an equal rating of +3 (very positive) on both topics. One may refer to his favourite newspaper in relation to other papers. The other refers to his best friend in the context of people he likes and dislikes. His personal involvement and investment is probably much greater in the second issue than on the first. Will he yield equally to persuasive messages on both issues? The social judgement theory of Sherif and Hovland (1961) has led to some research and an attempt to answer these questions. The theory postulates that a person's position on any attitude scale serves as an anchor from which he perceives and evaluates other positions on that attitude scale. If the communicator argues for a position that is close to receiver's, that position will be perceived as closer than it is in reality – assimilation. If the advocated position is rather distant from the anchored point it is seen as being even more distant – contrast. Statements within the assimilation area represent the latitude of acceptance and those outside it the latitude of rejection. What is of critical importance, according to this theory, is the width of the person's latitudes for the attitude in question. The smaller the latitude of acceptance, the greater the contrast effect, the less likely is his acceptance of the persuasive communication. Data from experiments (Hovland, Harvey and Sherif, 1957) support this analysis. What then are the variables that determine width of latitudes? The more extreme one's initial position and the greater the ego-involvement with the topic, the greater the latitude of rejection (Sherif, Sherif and Nebergall, 1965). In such cases the only way to effect persuasion to a widely discrepant position is to use a step by step technique; that is, to present each time a message that is near enough to that of the target person and then proceed to the next step, etc. They also found that on many issues a high credibility source will widen the latitude of acceptance and thus facilitate more attitude change. Maximum attitude change can therefore be expected where the target person does not hold an extreme attitude position, the issue is not ego-involving and the persuader has high credibility. Himmelfarb and Eagly (1974) make the point that the typical laboratory set-up involves a high credibility source and unimportant issues, and it is therefore no wonder that experimenters usually obtain attitude change. Hovland (1959) made the important point that these factors constitute differences obtained between laboratory and field studies. In field studies the issues matter to the people concerned, and these people are not students faced with the authority of an academic. There are, however, many real-life situations, teacher–pupil or doctor–patient interactions, in which there is high credibility of source *but* important attitudes are at stake which one is attempting to change.

To return to the question of high ego-involvement, Himmelfarb and Eagly, criticize Hovland's lack of clear definition of the term. He defined it as an attitude which is related to the individual's self-concept. The way, however, in which this variable has been manipulated in the experiments has not really clarified the term. Hovland, Harvey and Sherif used subjects who belonged to a group known for their strong views on the topic in question. Zimbardo (1960) informed subjects that their opinion on the topic was an indication of a personality factor. Miller (1965), on the other hand, manipulated high involvement by informing subjects directly of the importance of the topic to them and that their opinion was important as the enquiry was government-sponsored, and might have an effect on their policy. Miller's experiment is important for two reasons. His manipulation of ego-involvement has face validity in that it is made salient to the person and is made to have consequences for others. Furthermore it puts the emphasis on factors that others have found important (Kelman and Baron, 1974; Bramel, 1968). It also ties up with results from dissonance theory researchers, who have stressed the importance of a behavioural act that may have consequences for others, to the subject's maintenance of that attitude (Collins and Hoyt, 1972). The second point that emerges from Miller's experiment is that manipulation of ego-involvement leads to more extreme attitudes on these topics. It therefore appears that it is this double factor, of high ego-involvement and holding an extreme attitude, which causes the greatest resistance to persuasion. One final comment may be appropriate on this research topic. We speak of people that are prejudiced, intolerant and who see things in contrasts of black and white. It is easy to be tolerant about someone else's attitudes when one is not involved in an issue and does not hold an extreme attitude – in such a case one's latitude of acceptance is wide. What happens to us 'tolerant' people when *we* feel strongly about an issue – or have we stopped doing so?

Personality and susceptibility to persuasion

In this section, in which we deal with personal characteristics in persuasibility, we refer to the possibility that some people are more easily persuaded than others, irrespective of the topic in question or other factors like source and message variables.

We shall not be concerned with conformity to social influence within a group setting as this has been discussed in Chapter 4. Furthermore in the previous chapter in the context of the acquisition of attitudes, we dealt with the authoritarian personality, dogmatism and prejudice, and these were seen to be relevant also to attitude change. We shall limit ourselves to issues which are more specific to personality and persuasibility.

In his review of this area, McGuire (1968) points out that there 'is abundant evidence that persuasibility on one issue is positively related to persuasibility by the messages on other issues.' This has been shown in a study by Janis and Field (1956) in which they varied the source and also kind of topic. They report a significant underlying factor of persuasibility as a personality variable. When it comes to a breakdown of this general factor into more specific predictions there does not seem to be any clear evidence for such a relationship. Persuability does not seem to be related to such variables as intelligence, anxiety and self-esteem. To understand why there appears to be contradictory results on these personality factors and persuasibility, McGuire makes two important points. The first is that persuasion is mediated by at least two components: (a) comprehension, and (b) yielding. The relevance of this can be seen in studies on intelligence. Common sense would probably predict a negative relationship between intelligence and persuasibility, since the more intelligent person would have more confidence in his own opinion and could quickly think of counter arguments to the message. Some experimental findings tend to support this view, yet others either find no relationship or even a positive relationship between intelligence and persuasibility (Hilgard, 1965; Janis and Hovland, 1959). McGuire's point is, that the comprehension component is likely to be positively related to intelligence and therefore could favour attitude change. A simple persuasive argument would highlight *yielding*; with a complex one *comprehension* may be decisive. A similar point can be made about the anxiety variable. The anxious person may be less confident and therefore yield more easily but at the same time he may also be more preoccupied with his own thoughts and fears and therefore attend less to the persuasive message. This may be the reason why researchers have found conflicting results between anxiety and persuasibility

The second important contribution of McGuire on this topic is especially relevant to variables like anxiety and self-esteem. He points out that there are two distinct approaches to the question. We can administer some test of anxiety or self-esteem to subjects and subsequently expose them to a persuasive message. We can then see whether there is any correlation between the *chronic* personality variable and persuasibility. Alternatively we may manipulate the independent variable by inducing anxiety or self-esteem in half the group and follow this with a persuasive message. If the manipulated (acute) group was more or less persuaded than the control group, one could deduce a *causal* relationship between the *acute* personality factor and persuasibility. What is important is that the two are not confused. In the first place, an *anxious person* has learnt over time to cope with life in a specific way, which may be very different from a non-anxious person who has just been made anxious in the experiment. In the second place one has serious doubt whether the same terms are applicable in the two conditions. Take as an example the personality factor of self-esteem. In the 'chronic' condition a person is likely to fill in a questionnaire which is related to clinical observations of ability to cope and a general low self-evaluation. In the manipulated acute condition, low self-esteem has been induced by telling subjects that they have failed on many trials on a prior test (Mausner and Block, 1957). Failure induction can be totally different from chronic low self-esteem. A person that has failed on a number of tasks may attribute his failure to a variety of circumstances, which need not lower his real self-esteem. The person with chronic low self-esteem, however, is likely to view any new encounter as related to his perceived self. We have elaborated this point made by McGuire because of its general importance, beyond the topic of persuasibility. It is relevant to the general question of manipulating person factors within the laboratory situation (Aronson and Carlsmith, 1968). It also should put one on guard against the confusion between situational and personality factors in general.

In this review of the research originating from the Hovland–Yale school we did not find any grand theorizing, nor very general conclusions. Instead we have observed a painstaking search for independent variables that may account for attitude change. In this search, one often finds that the simple hypothesis has to be qualified and becomes more complex as it becomes evident that the single variable is confounded with others.

7
Cognitive consistency theory and attitude change

Within the domains of attitude change, social psychology has drawn heavily on the concept of *cognitive consistency* (see B1). All consistency models share the basic assumption that an individual tends to avoid cognitive inconsistency. Thus, if inconsistency occurs, various mechanisms are brought into play in order to reduce the inconsistency. The theory attracting the greatest amount of attention and experimental work is the theory of cognitive dissonance. Indeed, Insko (1967) has contended that 'judging from the amount of literature, dissonance theory appears to be the single most popular theory in the field of attitude change'. Hence, in the present chapter, no attempt will be made to outline all consistency theories. Rather, a detailed description of Festinger's (1957) theory of cognitive dissonance will be presented, with a critical analysis of its present position in the light of recent experimental work and some competing theories.

From the above quotation it is evident that it would be impossible to outline all the experimental data concerned with dissonance theory and so the focus will be held on illustrative data and on those experiments that have been the centre of some theoretical controversy. Finally, an attempt will be made to evaluate the original description of the theory in terms of its present status, and modifications which have been held necessary by its critics.

In 1957, Festinger outlined his theory of dissonance based on the premise that an individual will strive towards consistency within himself. Humans are seen as not tolerating inconsistency, and when it occurs, for example, when an individual believes in one thing and yet acts contrary to this belief, he is motivated to reduce the conflict. This conflict or inconsistency is called dissonance. Festinger defines this state of dissonance thus: 'two elements are in dissonant relation if, considering these two alone, the obverse of one element would follow from the other'. By a cognitive element, Festinger means a piece of knowledge, belief or opinion either about the environment or oneself. These cognitive elements can be in one of three relationships – dissonant, consonant or irrelevant. Thus, if a man believes that smoking is harmful but continues to smoke, these two cognitions are in a *dissonant* relationship. However, if whilst holding this view about smoking, he ceases to smoke, a *consonant* relationship exists. If he considers smoking harmful and at the same time knows he washes his car every Sunday, these elements are obviously in an *irrelevant* relationship.

The magnitude of any dissonance generated is a function of the following conceptual variables: firstly, the *importance* of each of the dissonant and cognitive elements. Thus if an opinion has little importance, behaviour inconsistent with this opinion creates relatively little dissonance: the obverse also holds. The second variable is that the amount of dissonance is a function of the *number* of dissonant and consonant cognitions which exist at that time. That is to say, the greater the ratio of dissonant to consonant elements, the greater the felt dissonance. Finally, dissonance is also a function of the cognitive *overlap*, i.e. the functional equivalence of the objects or activities represented by each cognition. Hence, the less two events have in common, the greater the dissonance. An example of this would be if a boy had to choose between buying a book or going fishing: more dissonance would be created than if he had to choose between going to the cinema or to the circus. Festinger also sets an upper limit to the amount of dissonance existing between two elements as being equal to the resistance to change of the less resistant of the elements. If the dissonance is magnified beyond this point, the less resistant element will be changed to conform with the other. Dissonance is thus reduced.

Festinger amplifies his general statement by discussing the theory's implications for a number of situations, which include specifically a decision-making process. One can see by the examples above that dissonance is often created in choice or decision situations. These may be divided into 'free choice' situations (Brehm and Cohen, 1962), and 'forced compliance' situations. It must be noted that all decisions involve conflict before resolution; after, and only after, resolution, can dissonance be said to exist, i.e. post-decisional conflict.

We will now look at some of the parameters of dissonance within the above two situations, beginning with those within free choice situations, i.e. those containing a choice between two or more positive alternatives.

Obviously, a decision to choose one alternative that is as desirable as another must give rise to dissonance, and thus give rise to pressures to reduce it. Reduction of dissonance can take one or more of four possible forms. The individual can revoke the decision, for example, if he has encountered subsequent information that alters the formulation of the decision, thus returning the individual to the original position. This method of reduction is often not plausible, and so an alternative method is to increase the attractiveness of the chosen item and decrease the attractiveness of the rejected item. This can often be accomplished by gathering information or support for the decision subsequent to that decision. Fourthly, one can increase the cognitive overlap between the choice items. This can be seen if, for example, the boy described above decided that both a book and going fishing are types of relaxation.

Brehm (1966) experimentally tested the hypotheses that (a) dissonance should be reduced by decreasing the attractiveness of the rejected items; and (b) that exposure to relevant information after the decision should also facilitate dissonance reduction. The results are only partially confirmatory but details of the experimental procedure will be given as they serve as a general model for many subsequent experiments.

Brehm used female subjects, who were asked to rate the desirability of several household items. The rationale given to the subjects was that the manufacturers wanted consumer reactions and would pay the subjects by allowing them to have

felt less need to call the obviously boring task enjoyable; this is reflected in the subsequent attitudes towards the task.

The above two experiments have been described in some detail because, after completing the outline of Festinger's theory, we shall see how they played a central role in a great deal of theoretical controversy. However, one must look at those people who will not engage in counter-attitudinal behaviour. Festinger contends that if such an individual does not succumb, dissonance is still felt in amounts according to the amount of punishments or rewards and the importance of the behaviour to be changed. Thus the greater the reward or punishment and the less important the behaviour, the more dissonance created. In illustration, consider a man who refuses a large amount of money to say he likes sweets. He would feel more dissonance than if the amount of money was small, or if he had been asked to act counter to his religious beliefs. One must note here that the relative importance of the behaviour is probably aligned to the centrality of the connected values (discussed further in Chapter 2).

It follows logically that in order to reduce the dissonance created from lack of compliance, one can magnify the importance of the resistant opinion or behaviour, or effectively reduce the magnitude of the reward or punishment.

It is difficult to find an explicit statement by Festinger on the difference between the free choice and the forced compliance situation, but Insko (1967) has conceptualized them within classic conflict language (see D2). Thus, free choice is seen as an approach–approach conflict (choice between equally pleasant alternatives) or approach–avoidance conflict where one is forced into behaviour which has at once rewarding and punishing consequences (one receives a reward, but 'accepts' attitudes counter to one's own). Thus, Insko is suggesting that the difference lies in the type of conflict from which the decision results.

It has been previously suggested that there are certain conditions under which the individual will actively seek out information. In the presence of a dissonant relationship, reduction of dissonance may take the form of seeking information which adds a new consonant element to the relationship. If the amount of dissonance is small, there would be correspondingly little searching for consonant information or avoidance of that information which increased the dissonance.

The amount of seeking for consonant information is directly related to the amount of dissonance, likewise the avoidance of information which adds to the dissonance. For example, consider a man who has just bought a new car. The decision was hard because many types of cars were equally as attractive. Having made the decision, he still holds some dissonant cognitions in the form of these other cars. According to the amount of dissonance, he will seek information which is in favour of his chosen car whilst avoiding information favourable to the other types of cars, in order to reduce the 'conflict'.

Also, from Festinger's formulation, if dissonance is extremely high (remembering that the extent of dissonance is limited to the total resistance to change of the less resistant element), the individual may well actively seek out dissonant information in order to push dissonance to the limit, force the least dissonant element to change, ultimately reducing dissonance. Now consider a man who believes very strongly that one should act fairly towards everybody. If he is in a position at work where he has to undermine other people's positions in order to gain promotion, dissonance of a high degree occurs. He might then seek out information on the efficacy of competition, the need for promotion for his family's sake and so on, in order to increase the dissonance to its limit. In this case, the least resistant element (the belief about treating others fairly) will change, and dissonance will be reduced.

However, one cannot always choose what information one is exposed to. For example, the influence of the mass media is so wide that one cannot predict and thus seek or avoid the information one comes into contact with. Such information is obviously capable of both reducing and promoting dissonance. In this instance a choice or decision is not a necessary condition for the production of dissonance, in that one is merely exposed to information contradictory to previously held cognitions. In this situation, one can reduce dissonance by one of several mechanisms. One can easily give an example to illustrate these. If an individual believes in ghosts and by chance hears someone on the television expounding a scientific theory against the existence of such a supernatural apparition, he may misinterpret the information given as consonant with his own views; he may question the credibility of the speaker; he may turn off the television; or he may simply change his opinions.

Festinger (1957, 1964) cites much experimental evidence on

the effect of voluntary exposure to information. He contends that much of the data can be interpreted within a dissonance framework, whilst admitting that much of it is 'causally equivocal and cannot be regarded as providing strong corroboration for the theory of dissonance' – the data on involuntary exposure being seen as more adequate. Festinger also sees the social group as an enormous source of both reduction and creation of dissonance. One may often go to a group expecting addition of consonant elements in a postdecision situation and find, on the contrary, that it produces more dissonance. Obviously, such things as the attractiveness and credibility of the disputing person and the importance of the issues involved also play an important part. The individual is then motivated to reduce his felt dissonance and this may result in his changing his opinion or attempting to change the other's opinion. He may also increase the perception of the other person as being boring, stupid, or prejudiced.

The above description has been, of necessity, somewhat cursory; however, it will serve as a framework within which the nature of the controversies may be understood.

It appears, if one looks closely at the evidence, that the empirical data support dissonance theory, if somewhat ambiguously at times. However, even if dissonance theory can adequately predict the outcome of such experiments, it is by no means exclusive of other theories and their explanatory power in a similar experiment. To illustrate the point, one can look at the forced compliance studies cited and show how just one of the other theoretical viewpoints can be utilized.

Consider the Kelman study (see p. 75). Dissonance theory adequately explains the results. However, so too does incentive theory (Janis, Elms and Gilmore, 1965). Incentive theory states that as individuals engage in tasks involving counter-attitudinal behaviour, they indulge in what is known as 'biased scanning'. That is to say that increased saliency of formerly non-preferred attitudes leads to rehearsal of them. When a third cognition is introduced (i.e. incentive) biased scanning and rehearsal is greater, leading to greater attitude change. A direct relationship thus exists between incentive and attitude change, providing no negative affect is aroused (e.g. suspicion). Theoretically then, the two theories should have opposite predictions concerning the Kelman (1953) experiment, in that dissonance theory predicts less attitude change when the incentive is greater; and, conversely, incentive theory predicts that the greater the incentive the greater the attitude change. However, both manage to explain the results by insisting that, in the case of incentive theory, the group with only five tickets had more incentive, therefore more attitude change. Festinger on the other hand, claims that there was greater incentive to work if everyone were to receive a free ticket, thus diminishing the need to reduce dissonance by attitude change. So, theoreticallly they differ, but in practice they are the same.

Let us now look at the Festinger and Carlsmith (1959) experiment (see p. 76). Elms contended (Elms and Janis, 1965), in this case, that twenty dollars reward may have aroused negative feelings in the subjects, which would outweigh the incentive value and thus produce less change. Again it would seem that with a little *post hoc* thought, predictions would be similar. That is to say, one might assume that the negative feelings, in terms of suspicion, would flood out the usual predictions made by incentive theory. Elms and Janis, in an attempt to establish the nature of such negative affect, finally reduced it to two variables which would lead to contradictory predictions between the two theories. The first variable was *sponsorship*. Sponsorship entails the source of communication. Thus, in America, the Russian government would be seen as a negative sponsor, and the American government as a positive sponsor. Thus incentive theory assumes that positive sponsorship leads to greater attitude change; but dissonance theory predicts that because individuals, under negative sponsorship, have extra dissonant elements and are still engaging in counter-attitudinal behaviour, consonance must be attained through greater attitude change. Incentive theory predicts that positive sponsorship leads to greater attitude change; whereas dissonance theory predicts that, providing the subject is willing to role play, or indulge in counter-attitudinal behaviour, negative sponsorship leads to greater dissonance and greater attitude change. The second variable is one of commitment. Incentive theory predicts that attitude change will only occur with actual action, whereas dissonance theory states that commitment alone is sufficient to produce dissonance which, in turn, will change attitudes (to be discussed in greater detail later). Subsequently two definitive experiments were carried out (Janis and Gilmore, 1965; Elms and Janis, 1965) to test the operationalized forms of negative affect, and the results were consistent with the predictions of incentive theory.

Nonetheless, the two theories are still not categorically delineated. Carlsmith, on examining the data, contends that neither experiment created sufficient dissonance to induce attitude change and so the experiments were far from satisfactory in deciding between the two theories. It would appear that dissonance theory can always use such an excuse for counter-evidence, i.e. that insufficient dissonance has been aroused.

Other theoretical viewpoints have also been put forward. Bem (1965), for example, offers an alternative explanation of the forced compliance studies, which will be dealt with in the next chapter. Suffice it to say that he feels that 'dissonance' *per se* is by itself neither a necessary nor a sufficient explanation for these studies and that he 'eschews any reference to hypothetical internal processes, and seeks rather to account for the observed functional relations between current stimuli and responses in terms of the individual's past training history' (see B1, A3).

What then are the necessary modifications to dissonance theory to allow clear predictions which are at variance with any other theory? Brehm and Cohen (1962) have extended basic dissonance theory to encompass two important variables, those of *commitment and volition.*

Commitment occurs when an individual has made a choice between two alternatives. The role of commitment in dissonance theory is to aid in the specification of the psychological implication and in the specification of the ways in which an individual will attempt to reduce dissonance. Brehm and Cohen contend that if the individual is committed to a decision then dissonant elements later introduced will arouse dissonance and motivate reduction of dissanance. Also, if dissonance is experienced, reduction takes the form of changing the least resistant elements, and these elements are those which are not related to the commitment.

Brehm and Cohen also discuss the role of volition. Volition obviously implies control and responsibility for one's behaviour and is necessarily involved in a choice or decision. Thus, 'other things being equal', the greater the volition in a decision or choice the greater the dissonance. Brehm and Cohen state that both these factors are necessary for the arousal of dissonance a statement that, in part, Collins and Hoyt (1972) would agree with. Collins and Hoyt see another important factor for the arousal of dissonance which is not explicitly stated within formal dissonance theory. They contend that the individual must perceive his act as having serious consequences. Cooper and Worchel (1970) found that in a forced compliance situation, dissonance is only aroused if counter-attitudinal advocacy leads to perceived undesirable consequences. For example in the Festinger and Carlsmith experiment, dissonance would only occur if the subjects really believed that they had convinced others of the enjoyment of the task, and thus motivated them to perform what was, in reality, a really boring task.

Another distinction has been drawn by Kelman and Baron (1974) in connection with the dilemmas in which individuals might find themselves and the implications for dissonance theory. They suggest that a functional analysis of processes is mobilized, and the nature of these processes depends on the motivation the individual feels during that situation. Kelman and Baron delineate two types of dissonance, *moral* and *hedonic*.

Moral dissonance is created by counter-attitudinal behaviour where the attitude is related to a value, e.g. religion, ethics *etc.* Moral dissonance has implications for the individual's self concept, and manifests itself in a guilt reaction. In this case, more dissonance would be aroused by greater reward and less dissonance by greater effort. Hedonic dissonance, on the other hand, occurs when one performs a task which is intrinsically boring or unpleasant. It gives rise to a concern for profitableness, and thus greater dissonance is generated under conditions of low reward and high effort. For moral dissonance, there is logically a direct relationship between attractiveness of inducing agent and the attitude towards the issue; an inverse relationship exists in situations of hedonic dissonance, i.e. the more attractive the inducing agent, the more negative the attitude towards the issue.

Thus it can be seen that the two types of dissonance specify different situations and lead to different predictions. The point is valid, and the fact that dissonance theory treats the two as formally equivalent shows just how much further specification and modification is necessary within Festinger's original formulation. Festinger (1957) admits that clear predictions are difficult from dissonance theory. He states, 'the problem ... is, of course, one of independently identifying situations or circumstances which produce dissonance habitually'. One hopes that some of the modifications described above will clarify this. At present dissonance theory suffers from a lack of precise explanation and prediction, and involves its adherents in *post hoc* rationalization of experimental results.

Festinger also admits to the vagueness of the definition of dissonance, especially in how to denote, *a priori*, whether a relationship between two cognitive elements is dissonant or consonant. He feels that this vagueness is due to lack of empirical work at the time of writing. Insko, writing ten years later, evidently feels that this clarification is not yet forthcoming, despite the proliferation of research carried out. However, the present authors feel that some of the modifications outlined go some way towards alleviating this problem.

It should be mentioned that Festinger (1968) does not rigidly adhere to his theory, or any consistency or balance theory, as being the only useful one within the field of attitude change. He accepts that many approaches are valid. 'The processes of attitude formation, maintenance, and change are not simple. Dissonance plays an important role; so do learning and imitation and conflict and reactions.' However, he states 'If treated as precisely and specifically as possible, I believe the theory of cognitive dissonance will prove a useful explanatory and predictive device.' Although it seems that such specification is being attempted, the big question is if precise enough delineation of the variables operating can be attempted without an exact knowledge of an individual's value and attitude system in any given case.

In conclusion, it appears that dissonance theory generated an extremely large amount of literature, much of which has produced corroboration for the theory. However, an attempt has been made to show that the data has also created alternative explanations and modifications.

It has become elaborated by Brehm and Cohen (1962) to deal with the attitude change that follows discrepant behaviour within commitment and choice situations. However, it is undergoing 'shrinkage' (Himmelfarb, 1974) in that, for example, the important inverse relationship between attitude change and magnitude of incentive for counter-attitudinal role playing (as exemplified by the Festinger and Carlsmith study) is found only under strict and narrowly defined conditions (e.g. Cooper and Worchel, 1970). Another type of shrinkage that Himmelfarb discusses is centred on the formulation of alternative theories and explanations for the basic assumptions and phenomena dissonance theory sets out to explain. Although none of these alternatives can be said to 'disprove' the theory (e.g. Elms and Janis, 1965, and incentive theory), such alternatives must call into question the theory's unique and appropriate explanatory power and one must assume that a number of diverse differentiations (e.g. Kelman and Baron, 1974) and factors are acting within situations traditionally defined as those of cognitive dissonance.

8
Equilibrium and change

In Chapter 7, an overview was given of just one specific theory concerning the nature of attitudes and the changing of attitudes. We now turn to an attempt (though not an inclusive one) to delineate some other theories which are concerned with the stable states of attitudes, i.e. their structure and some of the sources which are perceived as being central to any change. These theories generally encompass the nature of disequilibrium and how such disequilibrium alters the nature and direction of both attitudes and values. In covering this area we hope to encompass the three major components which are generally agreed to form an attitude, that is, the affective, cognitive and behavioural aspects. Each approach outlined is somewhat idiosyncratic in that all the theorists concentrate on combinations of the components in different permutations, and hence the emphasis changes according to their predilections. Each theorist is also somewhat special in this emphasis and throws interesting light upon the problems contained within this area. Thus, Rokeach (1975) is concerned mainly with the nature of value systems and their implications for the self-concept with a view to changing them within an educative rather than a persuasive situation. Such a persuasive situation, which has been strictly defined, is the central interest of Osgood's theory when discussing cognitive imbalance as a source and motivation of change. A shift in emphasis is seen when looking at Rosenberg's (1956, 1960) work, where he formulates a theoretical view in which the arousal of cognitive–*affective* imbalance is seen as necessary in producing attitude change. Still within the affective–cognitive sphere, Abelson and Rosenberg (1958), who had worked independently on cognitive mapping of attitudes, formulated the relationship among cognitive elements in affect-laden situations.

Finally, we come to a very special case of the relationship between attitudes and behaviour as expounded by Bem. No actual theory of attitude change *per se* is suggested in this 'radical Skinnerian' (see A3, B1) approach in that there is no actual imbalance, but change does occur through a process of self-observation.

All the above approaches are well formulated and highly original. We shall try to present them in their basic form, omitting, for clarity's sake, the wealth of elaborations and hypotheses to which they have given rise. Each approach deserves more detailed exposition, but we can only touch briefly on the relevant experimental literature and must leave the reader to fill in the details for himself, using the references we have given.

Firstly then, we turn our attention to affective dissatisfaction as discussed by Rokeach (1973). Rokeach maintains that inconsistencies must, of necessity, exist within all cognitive systems and that these inconsistencies may exist below a level of awareness (due to defensive reactions of the individual). However, the more conscious these contradictions or inconsistencies are, and the more they implicate the individual's self-conception, the more likely they are to lead to effective attitude and behaviour change. Indeed, the concern with the link between inconsistencies and self-concept is absolutely central to Rokeach's thesis. Traditionally, the view is taken that any inconsistency within cognitions will motivate change (cf. Festinger in the previous chapter). But Rokeach contends: 'a contradiction within the cognitive system may be assumed to have no psychological import unless it implicates self-conceptions'. Thus inconsistency between two cognitive elements is not important, but inconsistency between cognitions about oneself is. It is the cognitions and how the action in a given situation is perceived and how this reflects on the self concept that determine, firstly, if the inconsistency is affectively felt and, secondly, if it will then lead to cognitive and behavioural changes.

Obviously, there are great individual differences in how an individual conceptualizes himself and thus any one set of inconsistencies will have differential motivational effects. Thus, to use Rokeach's example, let us consider a professor of psychology who prides himself on his logic. If this professor then finds out that his students find his lectures illogical, his self-concept is challenged and the inconsistency is great. Consider then a minister whose highest value is in his morality. The fact that his sermons are illogical is not particularly worrisome to him; but he would be very upset if his parishioners perceived him as immoral. Both of the above concern different violations of the self-concept.

Following from this, it can be seen that some contradictions are perceived as more important in that they implicate the self-concept to a larger degree. Thus Rokeach contends that inconsistencies among values are more 'uncomfortable' in that they are central to evaluating the self and others. Therefore, inconsistencies involving the most important values to any one individual are most important for cognitive and behavioural change because of the greater tension and hence motivation. Rokeach assumes that such contradictions are not merely psychological but are also logical.

What one then feels is a 'felt difficulty', that is to say a discrepancy between how one perceives oneself and the actual performance. For if the action does not live up to standards held up for oneself, an inconsistency occurs. This inconsistency is essentially affective rather than cognitive and is the basic motivation for all ensuing changes. Indeed, inconsistencies between cognitive elements may not lead to any change whatsoever in that they do not reflect upon any aspect of the individual's self-conception. Once this discrepancy is set up, there is high pressure to reduce it. This may *seem* relatively easy but is often very difficult due to the degree of complexity and strategies involving self-deception.

Self or affective dissatisfaction is a common enough experience and is seen in states of anxiety, alienation, conflict etc. Such diffuse dissatisfaction is often very difficult to deal with as the source of the dissatisfaction cannot be easily identified, and thus the individual rarely knows which cognitive or behavioural change is necessary for resolution of the conflict. It is in this state then that the individual will seek therapeutic guidance to direct him to the source (see F3).

If, however, the individual is able to locate the source of the dissatisfaction (however correctly or incorrectly), he will be then motivated to remove the tension by modifying some component or components of his belief system to make them compatible with his self conceptions. It must be noted that Rokeach draws a conceptual distinction between what is commonly called self-esteem and self-dissatisfaction. He sees the former as being a relatively stable level whilst the latter changes according to the situation.

So what then causes self-dissatisfaction and how can it be effectively reduced? Dissatisfaction is seen in issues mainly concerning competence or morality (Bramel, 1968). Competence issues are seen as those situations in which skill or lack of skill is displayed by the individual. Dissatisfaction can occur in issues of morality when the individual, for example, harms others or displays lack of impulse control. Dissatisfaction is felt when the individual does not match up his actions to his own standards and the way in which he would like to see himself. These standards are most rigorously formed through societal agencies via a system of rewards and punishments. Through a process of social comparison (e.g. Jones and Gerard, 1967) the individual can judge his and others' competence and morality, the end result being an affective continuum from self-satisfaction to self-dissatisfaction. It is when the social comparison ends in self-dissatisfaction that cognitive and behavioural changes begin.

So, how is this dissatisfaction reduced? One way is to deny or repress the conflict. However, when the inconsistency can no longer remain below the level of consciousness, something has to be changed. The usual assumption is that the change would occur in the less central component (i.e. the inconsistent attitude rather than the inconsistent value). However, under Rokeach's formulation, the motivation comes from the inconsistency with the self-conception. Thus if the value is inconsistent, it will be the one to change. Logically, if two attitudes or values are consistent with one another but both inconsistent with the self-concept, there would be pressure to change both even if, in the process, the two became more inconsistent with each other. Thus Rokeach proposes a hypothesis which is in direct contradiction with traditional consistency theory approaches (see for example, Osgood's 'pressure towards consistency' described later).

Thus then Rokeach's theory can be held in contra-distinction to many theorists in his field. He concentrates on value and value change rather than attitudes as having greater implications for the self-concept. He also argues that his theory is concerned with long-term rather than short-term changes as seen in other theorists' viewpoints. He also contends that the assumption that attitude change leads to behaviour change rests on shaky evidence, and that the value change–behaviour change link is far more important and central. Rokeach first theoretically and then empirically outlines methods for inducing long-term changes in cognition and behaviour. The experimental manipulations are somewhat complicated and the reader is referred to Rokeach (1973); Rokeach and Cockrane (1972) for details. Rokeach's approach will be treated theoretically at present. Rokeach sees unconscious contradictions as psychologically maladaptive and undesirable. Thus if one can expose the individual to information about his own belief system in order to make him aware of the inconsistency, it will facilitate motivation to change and achieve higher levels of competence and morality – even at the cost of a comfortable life. This information must be simple and unambiguous and provide data about attitudes and values and their relationships with the individual's self-concept. The illuminated contradictions must be seen as credible without awakening defensive reactions. The above is done, basically, by giving subjects information about their own belief systems as well as similar information about significant others. The subjects' attention is drawn to the relationships between these values and attitudes as well as the contradictions inherent therein. Thus, by implication, the subjects are shown the possibility of harbouring contradictions within their own system. Rokeach (1973) describes three experiments in which he does just this; he found that when directed at terminal values (i.e. 'end states of existence' both personal and social) these values became even more highly valued. Also, there were changes within the value system. A change (long-term) was also found in value related attitudes as well as behaviour change.

Rokeach presents fairly supportive evidence, and it must be seen that many social psychological theories are now looking at the self-concept as a reference, which had been hitherto virtually ignored. His novel approach with regard to the nature and importance of various inconsistencies is certainly both central and interesting. The point that inconsistencies need not necessarily lead to change is well taken, and in our next section we will see that such a view is not necessarily incompatible with others in that the definitions and limitations change with the theories.

We now turn to sources of inconsistency which are purely cognitive. Osgood and Tannenbaum's (1955) consistency theory is not expounded as a challenge to Rokeach's theory; indeed none of the theories described are put forward in any kind of competitive way; these authors have only offered their theory to account for the *attitude* change resulting from a given and narrowly defined communication situation. They attempt a precise model which can encompass quantification of the variables and relationships involved and hence the magnitude and direction of an adjustment to an inconsistency. The model was initially developed through Osgood, Suci and Tannenbaum's (1958) work on the measurement of meaning, using seven-point bipolar scales. These were called semantic differentials, and consisted of ratings of two antonymous adjectives separated by seven spaces (see p. 33). Many such ratings were summed and correlated, allowing for a factor analysis which showed the most heavily loaded factor to an evaluative factor due to the favourable/unfavourable component common to all antonyms (e.g. good–bad; sweet–sour etc.)

Osgood and Tannenbaum thus inferred the existence of the evaluative dimension i.e. one of attitude, and proposed that an attitude is one of several dimensions located in a space of 'total meaning'. The attitude objects are then located along a number of semantic dimensions such as active/passive or weak/strong but it is the location on the pro/con dimension that defines the evaluative nature of the attitude involved. Thus two individuals may have equally positive attitudes towards democracy, but one may view it as passive and the other as active.

In a stable state, Osgood and Tennenbaum assume that attitudes have a tendency towards maximal simplicity, i.e. they move towards maximal polarization on either the positive or negative side. However, this applies to single attitudes; it is when two attitudes are linked via an assertion that the main force of their theory comes into play. When such a link exists, the authors assert that there is a movement towards equilibrium or congruity in order to allow maximal simplicity. This then is their paradigm, where an identifiable source makes an assertion about some concept or object that brings them into an evaluative relationship. If two incompatible attitudes *do* exist within one cognitive system, then the theory perforce assumes that they have never been linked.

The assertions that link the source and object can be either associative (A likes B) or dissociative (A dislikes B). (The distinction between the two assertions however, remains unclear; indeed, Osgood, Suci and Tannerbaum (1958) have admitted that operational definitions of assertions are difficult to formulate.) Thus objects can be located on a 7 point bipolar scale (+3 to −3) and when two linked attitudes occupy different places on this scale, the total pressure to congruity is equal to the difference in evaluative scale units between them. Whether this eventual evaluation is positive or negative depends on the direction of the congruence. Osgood and Tannenbaum have formalized this, as with all their hypotheses, within a mathematical model which allows precise quantification of the ensuing direction and magnitude of change. From these predictive tools it can be seen that, in the move towards equilibrium, both objects do not change equally in evaluation. That is to say that the more polarized, judgement changes proportionally less than the less polarized judgement. In clarification let us look at Osgood's own example. Consider an associative link in the form of praise between President Ford (+1) and Castro (−2), the pressure towards congruity would then result in Ford (the less polarized) being evaluated at −1 and Castro (the more polarized) being evaluated at −1. However, when the two above objects are linked via a dissociative assertion, a paradoxical effect occurs in that both objects are evaluated more highly. If however, the positive object of evaluation is the most polarized (i.e. if President Ford were evaluated at +3) there would be a decreased evaluation of both.

The above gives a cursory overview of the main tenets of the cognitive congruity principle (the reader is referred to Osgood and Tannenbaum, 1958, for the mathematical definitions and further hypotheses). As Insko (1967) has stated, it remains an impressive attempt to state precisely and mathematically a number of propositions. The only weakness lies in the two *ad hoc* corrections which detract from the overall elegance. These corrections are those for incredulity and an assertion constant. The former applies to situations where two objects of widely different evaluation are linked with an associative assertion, or two nearly identical objects are linked via a dissociative assertion. The reaction from the receiver is thus likely to be 'I just don't believe it', and so the normally predicted changes in evaluations are invalid through this rejection. The latter correction (the assertion constant) was applied in order to accommodate for the fact that, in specific communications dealt with, it was the object rather than the source which absorbed the major portion of the assertion's force. These two corrections were necessary in the interests of generality, but do not follow logically from the original propositions. Thus the theory, given that it is limited in its theoretical variation to the effects of communication in a particular setting, gives an eloquent account of which variables trigger purely cognitive disequilibrium, and how this is resolved through a process of attitude change. It must be noted, however, that there is a number of responses to such disequilibrium which do not necessitate attitude change (Abelson, 1959).

We have thus far discussed two completely different approaches to the major theme of this chapter: Rokeach's self-conception as a referent, and the purely cognitive imbalance resulting from a communication. Where then does the affective component come into play and interact with cognition? It is true that when speaking about evaluations, affect must be present, but no direct relationship has been emphasized as yet.

We now look at Rosenberg's theory where the *affective–cognitive* imbalance is seen as a necessary condition of change. We will also consider the extension outlined by Rosenberg and Abelson and see how the two cater for different problems.

Rosenberg (1968) contends that his model is one of 'a radial structure model of intra-attitudinal balancing'. The basic assumption is that there is a consistency between a relatively stable affective or evaluative orientation towards an object and the person's beliefs about how that object is related to other objects of affective significance. Thus positively evaluated objects are seen as facilitating attainment of goals, having certain attributes, and as being grouped with other positively evaluated objects. These objects are distinct from negatively evaluated objects where the converse is true. Thus the sign and amount of attitudinal affect towards any given object is correlated with the overall positive or negative affective import of other related objects. Rosenberg focuses mainly on cognitions concerning the value-attaining and value-blocking function of objects in the class of advocated changes in public policy (Rosenberg, 1956).

Rosenberg asserts that attitude acquisition and change is composed of two distinct processes in that one can modify the affective component resulting in a change of the cognitive component and vice versa. He formalized it thus: One can modify the cognitive response, for example, in a communication situation where new beliefs are acquired. Each of these beliefs link the object to some 'locus of affect'. In proportion to the strength, number and consistency of these beliefs, there will be a similar, but tentative affective disposition toward the object in question. If no previous stable attitude exists, this then becomes the attitudinal affect. When previous attitudes do exist and the new beliefs either predominate or replace them, the resolution occurs by the old disposition giving way to the new. The second process is almost identical except that the affective response is modified and cognitions are tentatively adopted consistent with that affect.

These processes will operate only when the felt inconsistency over reaches the individual's tolerance limit (a poorly defined but necessary concept), and when the original alteration of either the affective or cognitive component has been compelling enough or is maintained to the point of being irreversible.

Attitude *change* is thus due to a sort of homeostatic mechanism in which the arousal of affective–cognitive inconsistency arouses 'further symbolic activity' towards restoration of inner consistency. If the inconsistency is above a tolerance limit then the attitude is unstable and reorganization occurs until (a) the communication is rejected, the original stability being restored; or (b) fragmentation occurs via isolation from each other of the inconsistent affective and cognitive components; or (c) attitude change (as seen in the two processes reported above).

Rosenberg (1968) sees his model as distinct from the later version developed by Abelson and Rosenberg. This theory is known as the 'symbolic psycho-logic' theory. The former model focusses, for any particular object, upon its relations with other objects. He asserts that attitude description, the induction of intra-attitudinal inconsistency, and the testing of predictions concerning methods of consistency resolution, can be pursued more readily within the earlier version. The symbolic psycho-logic approach focusses more upon a larger area of attitude–cognitive space where no one object is seen as central. The approach is to look at a large section of total space and the interaction between elements within it. This is called the 'conceptual arena' (Abelson and Rosenberg, 1958) within which cognitive units are connected via cognitive relations. These relations can be positive (e.g. 'likes'), negative (e.g. 'dislikes'), null (e.g. 'doesn't affect') or ambivalent (these are combinations of both positive and negative relations).

When an individual is motivated to think of his 'conceptual arena', he is guided by 'psycho-logical' rules (see Abelson and Rosenberg, 1958). Imbalance occurs when thought about the conceptual arena leads to the discovery of inconsistent or ambivalent relations. Once discovered, resolution must occur and this can take one of three forms. That is, (a) a change in one or more of the relations, (b) redefinition or differentiation of one or more of the elements, or (c) cessation in thinking about the inconsistency – the parallel is clear with the earlier version.

Again the reader is directed to the fact that this cannot be an explicit delineation of the two theoretical versions; merely an idea of the basic assumptions contained within the affective–cognitive approach. Both versions, singly, focus on the organization and achievement of further consistency; the earlier approach dealing with the relations of a single concept, while the psycho-logic approach focusses on the inner structure of the block of attitudinal space, that contains and gives equal prominence to each concept.

What, then, has this to do with behaviour *per se*? The theorists thus far have concentrated on internal consistency (even in Rokeach's case), the outcome of inconsistency being measured in scale-values on a paper and pencil test. How then does an attitude effect behaviour, or in terms of Bem's analysis, how does behaviour effect attitudes? We have already seen in Chapter 7, how Festinger has shown that embarking on counter attitudinal *behaviour* will effect a change in attitude. Bem offers an alternative theoretical explanation within a completely new conceptual framework. In contradistinction to the previous discussions, some experimental evidence will be presented in that Bem's theory and its critics revolve around his experimental demonstration of his central points.

Bem (1965) couches his whole thesis on a virtual redefinition of the terms previously used. He calls himself an 'unreconstructed behaviourist' as opposed to the reconstructed behaviourists, who, like Osgood, Suci and Tannenbaum use internal mediating responses. Further he defines at attitude as 'an individual self description of his affinities for and aversions to some identifiable aspect of his environment'. Thus the cognitive component is equated with self descriptive belief statements (verbal responses). The behavioural component is the individual's observations of himself (as seen in pencil and paper tests). Therefore, Bem asks, if these overt behaviours comprise the operational criteria of attitudes, why can they be used not as the conceptual definition of attitudes? His position on this question will become clear as we proceed with his argument.

Following Skinner (1957), the ability to respond differentially to one's own behaviour and its controlling variables is seen as a product of social interaction. The methods used to teach an individual to describe his own behaviour do not differ basically from those to teach him to describe other objects in his environment. According to Skinner's analysis, those self-descriptive statements which are assumed to be under the control of the individual do in fact remain under the control of the same public events which members of society use to infer individual states. It is thus not unusual, when asking someone if they are hungry, for that person to consult his watch. It also seems that internal control of an individual's self-descriptions can be replaced by external sources of control and information. For instance, consider the famous Schachter and Singer (1962) experiment, where subjects were given injections of adrenalin under various conditions which supplied them with the gross discrimination that they were feeling emotional; however, in order to discriminate the exact emotion, they referred to the actions of another (an experimentally manipulated stooge). This and e.g. Valins (1966) shows that external cues are used to categorize internal states *when that internal state is ambiguous.*

Bem takes the analysis one step further. He contends that one observes one's *own* behaviour to gauge one's internal states. Thus the by now famous example of the man when asked if he liked brown bread, replying 'I guess I do, I'm always eating it'. That is, the discriminative stimuli (cues) controlling the attitudinal statement are solely the individual's overt behaviour, and are functionally equivalent to the answer an outside observer would give in that he relies on the same evidence. Bem then contends that, logically, if one manipulates the individual's overt behaviour and the controlling conditions, one should be able to predict and control the attitudes the individual will hold.

He also extends this to cover how one infers the 'trueness' of one's own statements, that is, the amount of credibility one can attribute to one's own verbal behaviour. Again following Skinner, he distinguishes between 'mands', which are under the control of specific reinforcement contingencies (rewards and punishments), and 'tacts' – a descriptive statement which is under the control of some aspect of the environment (see A7). One must be able to distinguish these mand–tact characteristics in order to infer the truth. Obviously, if we knew that a famous person is endorsing a product because he was paid a vast amount of money, he is seen as manding and thus credibility is low. Bem assumes that we view our own verbal statements in the light of this analysis.

The above is a brief account of how attitudes are inferred in a steady and stable state. What then causes change? Bem has applied his arguments as an alternative explanation of a number of dissonance phenomena. His argument is illustrated in the paradigmatic case of forced compliance studies in which subjects wrote counter-attitudinal essays for varying amounts of monetary reward (see Ch. 7). The 'classical' finding, as mentioned before, is that subjects with little or no compensation express post-manipulation attitudes, which reflect agreement with the position taken in the essay. Those subjects with large amounts of compensation showed no significant change in attitudes from a control group, a phenomenon explained within a dissonance framework. If one reinterprets this in a self-perceptual view, are the results predictable? If one considers the behaviour from an outsider's point of view, one can see that in the low compensation group there is no question of writing an essay for financial gain, and thus we can assume something about the individual's attitudes i.e. he holds attitudes consistent with the essay. If the subjects were getting a large reward, one cannot infer anything about their attitudes, as the incentive is enough to elicit the behaviour. Therefore the observer's best guess is that the subjects' attitudes are consistent with those of randomly selected subjects.

So, the *actual* subjects in a forced compliance study are doing just this – acting as observers of their own behaviour and inferring the same attitudes. This was originally just an alternative statement, but Bem experimentally tested the analysis several times using a methodology now known as the 'interpersonal simulations'. Within this method, an observer–subject is given a description of one of the conditions of a dissonance experiment and asked to estimate the attitudes of the participating subjects. These observers' inferences were found to mirror the original dissonance findings.

Bem has been criticized in that no information was given to the observer subjects about the pre-manipulation attitude levels. He contends however, that this criticism is based on a 'misunderstanding' of the methodology in that the individual's attitude statements and an observers' judgements about the individual's attitudes are 'output statements' from the same 'initial program'. Both operate on the same self-selection rule i.e. 'What must my (this man's) attitude be if I am (he is) willing to behave in this fashion in this situation?' Thus if an individual actually arrives at his final attitude *via* the self-selection rule in a dissonance experiment, then any prior attitude has little salience for him in that the incoming behaviour updated his information on his attitudes. Therefore, as far as the individual is concerned, his post-manipulation attitude is the same as that which motivated him to comply at the beginning. Hence, there is *no attitude change per se*, phenomenologically speaking: Bem and McConnell (1970) simply asked the subjects what was their original attitude before the dissonance experiment. The subjects failed to recall and were thus unaware of any change.

This analysis is not offered as a confrontation or challenge to dissonance theory but merely as an alternative. Decisions between them are premature; indeed Bem doubts the possibility of a crucial experiment to decide between them. The interpretation appears to be sound and the methodology is sophisticated; the formulation certainly has much intuitive appeal and is an elegant conceptualization.

We have outlined four different approaches which present us not only with emphasis on different aspects of attitude/

value stability and change, but also with completely different conceptual distinctions. Osgood and Tannenbaum give a limited theory of attitude change within a defined situation, which presents a conceptualization of a rational evaluative categorization of objects within relation to each other. They adopt a mathematically analytic approach to predict imbalance and its resolution. Rosenberg, and Rosenberg and Abelson have offered another conception which includes affect to a much larger extent but still within such language as 'conceptual arenas' – totally confined to processes of balance in an assumed model. Rokeach on the other hand emphasizes not cognition, no affect in terms of balance, but a conceptualization of man weighing up the equilibrium between his values/attitudes/performance in direct relationship to the implications that they have for the self image. Finally, Bem has put forward another completely different approach within a behaviourist framework, where man is seen as referring to his overt actions in order to infer the attitudes he holds.

All of the above offer sound experimental evidence for their viewpoints. One might then ask, if all the evidence is equally distributed among all the theories, which one is right in terms of stability, disequilibrium and change in attitudes and values? Perhaps there is no answer. However, it seems from even this brief overview that the question of 'rightness' is not necessarily relevant here. Almost any monolithic theory of the processes involved must, almost by definition, be wrong; and in weighing up the subsequent chapter, it seems to be more appropriate to evaluate, both pragmatically and scientifically, how each approximates to 'rightness' according to the problems looked at – and the levels of problems vary tremendously from theory to theory.

9
Improving resistance to attitude change

In Chapter 6 we dealt with the problems of communication factors in enhancing attitude change, and some of the other chapters have touched on areas relating to ways of persuading individuals to embark on attitude discrepant behaviour, or change their attitudes towards objects, individuals, groups etc.

One would think that if the literature were sifted thoroughly enough and the research evaluated wisely, anyone who wished to control the way we feel about or perceive a given object, idea etc. could manipulate our attitudes as they pleased. Given this and the extensive technology evolved to enable such people to reach almost every individual, e.g. the mass media, literature and so on, one wonders how we have avoided being controlled and still manage to maintain some of our own attitudes. Indeed, one wonders how any minority or 'deviant' groups could exist. Of course, this is not to say that we are always unaffected by communications; some of the information is assimilated into our ongoing cognitive system, some is rejected, and some alters our attitudes. Nevertheless, resistance occurs; it has to occur or we would constantly sway with the prevailing persuasive communication, and under these circumstances no consistency in our behaviour or our attitudes would be possible.

So, given that resistance occurs, the questions when, why, how and under what conditions must be answered. The present chapter attempts an answer, although it is as well to understand that the above questions are not always so easily separable.

As McGuire (1964) has pointed out, resistance to persuasion cannot be seen as the inverse of the persuasion process itself. That is to say that one cannot look at the parameters which induce effective persuasion, minimize or invert them, and expect to produce resistance to the selfsame communications. By inverting the conditions of effective persuasive communications one could minimize the attitude change found, but this is not the total picture of what is meant by resistance.

In discussing the factors involved one must consider to some extent how general or specific any resistance may be. Thus, those personality traits related to rigidity, for example, may be seen as a predisposition the individual brings to bear on any attempt to persuade him; this is a general characteristic of that individual and will operate to some extent in any attitude change situation. The extent to which this predisposition creates resistance depends on other factors, but some initial resistance must be expected from such individuals.

If one looks at the structure of each individual's cognitive system, then there is a further factor which determines the amount of resistance in terms of the centrality of the attacked belief (Rokeach, 1960). Thus there seem to be at least three levels on which resistance might be expected to operate and be induced – the enduring characteristics or predispositions of the individual, the belief systems which can change, and the specific manipulations which as yet can only be well defined and utilized within an experimental procedure – although implications for the 'real world' are apparent.

Obviously, if an individual commits himself to a decision or an attitude, he will be resistant to changing that attitude especially if he has been *seen* to commit himself. Thus, whilst mere private decision can induce some resistance, public announcement of one's belief confers more resistance (Deutsch and Gerard, 1955). That is to say that if one decides privately that, for example, Negroes are inferior, one will resist attempts to show otherwise to some extent. However, if you announce your opinion of Negroes publicly, the commitment is that much larger and resistance is more extreme. If the same individual then takes active participation on the basis of that belief, i.e. one acts towards Negroes as if they were inferior, resistance is even greater. (Kelman, 1953). There are some conditions under which this commitment is more binding, for example, when the behaviour is elicited with the least pressure (King and Janis, 1956).

Rosenbaum has shown, also, that one's commitment to a belief 'externally' by being told someone else thinks one holds that belief results in an increased adherence to the belief. It is a mild effect, but discernible.

Another approach to increasing resistance to persuasion has much in common with the basic assumptions of the balance theorists. If one can anchor the attacked belief to already held cognitions, or at least sensitize the individual that such links exist, it becomes difficult to change that belief, since this would involve changing a whole network of beliefs or endurance of cognitive inconsistency which is both uncomfortable and difficult. If one links such an attacked belief to another accepted value, the belief remains resistant to the extent that it is perceived as being instrumental to the attainment of a positively valued goal and/or facilitating avoidance of a negatively valued goal (Rosenberg, 1956; Zajonc, 1960). In this way one could conceptualize of a manipulation that accentuated these linkages before delivery of a persuasive communication, and one would expect resistance to occur.

McGuire (1964) has discussed the 'Socratic effect' in this context. He suggests that merely asking subjects to rehearse related beliefs which he holds, makes these linkages more salient to the initial belief and thus lends enhanced resistance to subsequent attacks – at least to the extent that such attacks will introduce inconsistencies into the individual's belief system.

It will have become apparent from the discussion in Chapter 6 that the source of a message can also produce resistance to the message communicated. That is to say that by tying a belief to positively valenced sources, for example by pointing out that the opinion is held by others that the individual values highly, will lead to resistance to changing that belief. Schachter and Hall (1952) have shown that even anonymous groups and individuals can confer such resistance if the believer is made to recognize that such groups or individuals share his belief.

The above 'anchoring' approaches can be utilized as pretreatments to persuasive communications and can be tailored specifically to the areas of belief which would come under attack. The ensuing resistance is basically brought about in one of two ways. Firstly, the individual to be persuaded can be provided with new information which connects the belief to other, already held cognitions. Secondly, one can work within the individual's existing cognitive system making linkages more salient.

As mentioned before, the type of belief attacked confers varying degrees of resistance. This resistance lies in the nature of the belief rather than in any pretreatment designed to arouse it. Rokeach (1963) encompasses this in his notion of centrality. This notion rests on three simple but basic assumptions: first, not all beliefs are as important as others to any one individual; thus the individual beliefs in any system vary along a central-peripheral dimension. Second, the more central a belief is, the more resistant it will be to change. Third, if a change occurs to a central belief, it has very widespread repercussions in the rest of the belief system. One might expect from this, that the central beliefs of each individual will be purely idiosyncratic. However, Rokeach assumes that beliefs are social in nature, and thus defines central or primitive beliefs as 'uncontroversial beliefs supported by a unanimous social consensus among those in a position to know'. We will see later that this definition of centrality is almost analogous to McGuire's usage of 'cultural truisms', although the latter is more superficial. Rokeach continues to point out that these central beliefs represent basic truths about physical reality, social reality, and the nature of the self; they are a subsystem within the total system in which the person is most heavily committed. Violation of these primitive beliefs supported by unanimous consensus may lead to severe disruptions of beliefs about one's self-identity and can call into question one's competence to cope – or even one's sanity. It can be seen that, since violent consequences can result upon questioning these central beliefs, such beliefs will be very resistant to change in most circumstances.

Rokeach (1960) reports an investigation by Zavala in which he presented nine statements some of which were primitive belief statements, some authority belief statements (less central) and some peripheral belief statements. The subjects were asked to rank the statements in terms of which they were most reluctant to relinquish, and so on. The three primitive beliefs were found to be most resistant to change, followed by the authority beliefs and finally the peripheral beliefs. It is interesting to note that the majority of the subjects adhere to primitive beliefs with absolute intensity (i.e. within the 92–98 per cent range). Presumably, following the literature cited previously, if one wanted to give specific pretreatments to enhance resistance, an extremely efficient way would be to link the attacked belief to one of these central beliefs. When any central belief is called into question, an emotional disturbance is likely to ensue, as we have already said. In the Asch 1956) experiments on conformity (see, too, B1), several stooges called into question a central belief about physical reality, i.e. they reported, in the presence of a subject, that two unequal lines were equal. The resulting anxiety in the subject was apparent; however, it is interesting that many of the subjects succumbed to the pressure and agreed with a decision which was blatantly opposite to the perceived physical reality. The question is, was the central belief changed or was it a case of compliance in order to reduce tension? The question is a difficult one to answer; to change a central belief is hard as it means altering the whole system of beliefs connected to that one; but on the other hand, mere overt compliance should create inconsistency, and thus produce as much psychological discomfort as being at variance with other people's judgement.

So far, the discussion has been rather general, concerning itself with a description of the type of factors which control the amount of resistance created. We now turn to a theory which concerns itself solely with the problems of selecting different treatments which will increase resistance to any subsequent attack. We will deal with the particular theory in detail as it is unique in its approach. Later we will suggest other ideas connected with this and also try to answer one of the original questions of why resistance occurs.

The inoculation approach (McGuire, 1962a; 1964)

This approach stems originally from a biological analogy. When inoculated an individual is made resistant to some attacking virus by pre-exposure to a weakened form of the same virus. This weakened form stimulates the individual's defences against the stronger form but is not, itself, strong enough to become the disease. McGuire extrapolates this process to a persuasion situation. He argues that, from the biological analogy, there are two ways of resisting counter-attitudinal propaganda. These are, firstly, making the attitude 'healthier' by providing the individual with supportive information and arguments and, secondly, by the process of inoculation described above. If the individual has been living in an environment where his attitudes have not yet been threatened, McGuire maintains that the latter approach should be superior. In order to see if this is so, McGuire had to find some attitudes which have existed in a 'germ-free' environment, that is, those attitudes which have not been previously attacked. Thus he uses 'cultural truisms', i.e. beliefs that are so widely shared by others in the individual's social and cultural milieu that he will have never heard them attacked.

Of course, according to the selective exposure postulate discussed in Chapter 7, one could argue that all attitudes should be relatively free from previous attacks. Individuals should defensively avoid encountering counter attitudinal information and thus their attitude should remain 'healthy'. However, McGuire uses cultural truisms in order to ensure that the attitudes have been maintained in a 'germ-free' environment. He found that many such truisms were concerned with health matters. He gave many statements such as 'mental illness is not contagious' and 'the effects of penicillin have been, almost without exception, of great benefit to mankind' to a number of students, who were asked to rate their amount of agreement on a fifteen-point scale, thus finding those statements with the unanimous agreement within that culture.

McGuire postulates that, having found these truisms, the connected attitudes are extremely vulnerable to attack. This vulnerability stems from two sources. Firstly, the individual lacks practice in defending these truisms as they are so seldom attacked. Secondly, there is a lack of motivation to defend them because they were held to be unassailable and thus not necessitating any defence. If this is so, inoculation in the form of a weakened argument should provide the individual with just enough threat to motivate him to practise counter arguments whilst not being so strong that it acts as a completely refuting argument.

Within his theory he has experimentally distinguished and investigated three defensive variables which are important in assessing the efficacy of the pre-treatment. These variables are (a) the amount of threat contained within the initial defence.

Obviously, as with biological inoculation, too much threat would merely bring on the very disease one hopes to resist. (b) The amount of active participation in the defences required of the attacked individuals. (c) The optimum amount of time between the defence and the real attack of the truism.

We will look at these three in slightly greater detail as much of McGuire's later experimental work rests on understanding his conceptualizations.

For manipulation of the threat content, McGuire uses two basic types of defences, supportive and refutational. That is, arguments favourable towards the truism (hence non-threatening), and arguments which are immediately followed by refutations of those arguments. By analogy, one can see how these two types correspond to supportive therapy and inoculation. McGuire further distinguishes two subtypes of refutational defences: refutational–same defences are those in which the same arguments are presented and refuted as those which form the subsequent attack; refutational–different defences are those in which different arguments and refutations are presented from those which form the subsequent attack.

The amount of active participation in the inoculation is manipulated in such a way that there is an active and passive condition. In the passive condition, the subjects are asked to read a defensive essay already prepared for them. In the active condition, subjects write their own defensive essay. Obviously, in the latter case, some help is given as the subjects, by definition, do not know what sort of arguments and counter arguments are relevant to a cultural truism. This manipulation provides practice and motivation by the nature of the task.

The time variable is looked at in order to ascertain the optimum amount needed as immunity may take time to build up or may decay if too long a period is allowed. Hence McGuire's studies vary from a time limit of several minutes to one week.

We will now look at some of the research in greater detail, thus allowing an evaluation and an exposition of some of the subsidiary hypotheses McGuire has formulated. First we will review experiments concerning refutational and supportive defences. A refutational defence should provide greater resistance to subsequent attacking arguments than a supportive defence by nature of the process of inoculation and immunization.

McGuire has used both passive and active defences in his investigations.

McGuire & Papegeorgis' (1961) study will be described in some detail as it will serve as a paradigm in which to understand experiments presented later. They argue that refutation–same defences produce greater resistance to subsequent arguments than do supportive defences. The procedure was as follows. Subjects were given two one-hour sessions which were forty-eight hours apart. In the first session they were exposed to supportive and refutational defences, and in the second session they were exposed to the attacking arguments. The defences consisted of writing essays defending one truism, and reading a thousand-word essay defending another. One manipulation was concerned with whether subjects used outlines (in writing condition) or underlined key sentences (in reading condition). A second manipulation was whether both the defences were supportive or both refutational. At the end of the first session, subjects were given a questionnaire measuring their belief on the four truisms.

In the second session, subjects read and underlined key sentences contained in attacks against three truisms, including the two that had been previously defended. Subjects were then asked to fill out a comprehension task and a belief questionnaire.

Although somewhat complicated, the above design exemplified the sophistication which is apparent in all McGuire's investigation and which is one of the characteristics of this theory in general. The results from the above experiment will be detailed in table form. The means given are from a fifteen-point belief scale given to the subjects.

Type of defence	*Mean*
Neither attack nor defended	12.62
Attack only	6.64
Refutational	10.33
Supportive	7.39

The predicted effect was found. It is noticed that after the *first* session, the supportive defences immediately strengthened the belief more than the refutational defences (although not reaching statistical significance) but this breaks down after the attack is presented. McGuire calls this immediate strengthening the 'paper-tiger' phenomenon.

The above authors, in a further study, also found that refutational-different defences are as effective as refutational-same defences as presented in the above investigation. In line with the inoculation approach one would expect this, as any threat is seen capable of motivating the individual to acquire belief bolstering material.

The data is not clear as to whether refutational defences are superior to supportive defences when the attack follows immediately after the defences, however (Anderson and McGuire, 1965). It *is* clear, though, that with a delay between defence and attack both refutation-same and refutation-different defences are superior to supportive ones. This is required by inoculation theory if it is to hold true, as the threatening component must act and be instrumental in producing the immunizing effect (McGuire, 1964).

In discussing the active/passive component, one would assume from the motivation and practice hypothesis that an active condition would be superior to a passive condition, in that it involves the subject and motivates him to think about and practise counter-arguments. Paradoxically, McGuire contends that subjects perform so poorly in an active condition, due to their lack of practice, that they gain little from the exercise. Thus the active condition gains strength purely from the motivational aspect. Passive defences, on the other hand, gain strength from first immersing the individual in the relevant material and secondly, with refutational defences at least, motivating the individual to bolster his defences. Thus McGuire postulates that passive defences should confer more resistance to persuasion. This postulate is expanded into a number of subsidiary hypotheses. Insko (1967) comments that 'The research ... is remarkably supportive of the hypotheses. One cannot help but be impressed with McGuire's ability to intuit and empirically support non-obvious predictions.' However, the active/passive dichotomy does not logically follow from the biological analogy and Insko continues, 'It is therefore legitimate to ask to what extent McGuire is listing one coherent theory as opposed to a miscellaneous collection of explicit and implicit assumptions.' However, McGuire cannot be faulted if evaluated from a pragmatic approach.

McGuire develops his theory so that it has implications concerning various sequences and combinations of defences, an excellent review of which can be found in McGuire (1964).

In the question of persistence over time, the process of defensive resistance is quite complex, and there are many other factors apparently operating besides those discussed in inoculation theory. Other theories may thus prove complementary rather than denying the operation of those mechanisms described in inoculation.

As to one of our original questions – will inoculation work outside a 'germ-free' environment – this remains to be tested. McGuire is dubious, but some modification may provide a more general approach to the problem of resistance to persuasion.

One different approach has been suggested by Tannenbaum (1967) in the framework of the congruity principle as discussed in Chapter 8. Congruity exists when attitudes towards both the source of the message and the concept are favourable, and when the direction of the assertion is likewise favourable. Incongruity exists when these are not in line and a tension is thus created to change the attitude toward the objects of judgement involved. Tannenbaum admits that where resistance to change occurs, his work closely parallels McGuire's theory. He uses the same experimental procedure as McGuire, but hypothesizes different mechanisms to account for the results. The work of the congruity theorists on resistance centre mainly on a situation in which the main attack on the beliefs consists of a favourably evaluated source making a strongly negative assertion against a favourably evaluated concept, the prediction being a negative shift in the attitude toward the concept. Tannenbaum (1966) investigated four strategies for eliminating this shift using McGuire's 'cultural truisms'. These four were, denial, source derogation, refutation and concept boost (see below).

The rationale underlying these is as follows: Incongruity only arises when cognitive elements are brought into an evaluative relationship *via* an assertion. Therefore, if one can dissociate the source and concept, severing the negative link (via *denial*) between them in the main attack message, then the degree of incongruity and hence the pressure towards change, should be reduced. That is, if one refuses to recognize the link between the source and the concept, then no incongruity can exist. Likewise, if one were to make the source become negative in evaluation (*source derogation*), this would also lessen incongruity and pressure towards change. Thirdly, one could change the importance of the message, that is, by questioning the validity of the assertion or rebut or reverse the salient points of the attack (*refutation*) one could weaken the amount of attitude change. Finally, the total pressure towards change in an incongruent situation is not distributed in inverse proportions to the respective intensities of the original attitudes toward source and concept. Thus the more intense attitudes are less susceptible than the weaker ones (Tannenbaum, 1956). Hence, if one makes the original attitude stronger (*concept boost*) it should be more resistant to change. This is similar to McGuire's supportive defence, and showed great resistance in contra-distinction to McGuire's results. However, in general by investigating different combinations of the above, the refutation strategy is consistently superior as a persuasion reducer – which corroborates McGuire. Thus, although the results agree with those of McGuire, the postulated mechanisms differ. Evidence for inoculation theory is formidable but also circumstantial (McCaulay, 1965), and Tannenbaum feels that in many of McGuire's studies the assertion-weakening characteristics can account for much of the data as readily as the threat-providing aspect of inoculation. (He also admits that the converse is true.)

A further way of looking at communication-induced resistance effects is from the point of view of *information integration theory* (Anderson, 1968, 1971) and represents another useful but disparate approach to this problem. The theory assumes that the attitudinal response to several messages is a weighted average of the scale values of the messages plus the recipient's initial attitude on the issue. (The weight represents the psychological influence on the individual and depends on the parameters of the communication and personality situation). Therefore if a message of low-polarity is introduced prior to a more polarized message, the result can be a lower-polarized attitude than if the recipient had been exposed only to be a more polarized attitude i.e. resistance (Himmelfarb, 1974), although it results from information integration rather than from an active process of opposition to the second communication. The theory is not denying that active resistance can occur, as in McGuire's inoculation procedure or in response to inconsistent or contradictory information between communications. This active resistance should result in a change of weighting of the communication, but a distinction must be drawn between a lowered attitude which results from an integration of communications of different polarities and one which results from a decrease in persuasiveness of a particular communications. Integration theory can detect each difference.

We have, up till now, looked at resistance implicit in the individual's cognitive structure (Rokeach, Rosenbaum etc.), prior training in resisting persuasive attempts (McGuire, Tannenbaum) and at least one way of distinguishing different types of resistance. However, one can also induce a generally resistant cognitive state. Personality, motivational and ideological states are correlated with resistance to social influence pressures, and can be induced or brought to bear on a given situation. Such factors as authoritarianism (Adorno *et al*, 1953), and persuasibility and self esteem (Cohen, 1959) can account for the amount of resistance brought into a persuasion situation by the individual – although the generality of these have been called into question (Janis and Field, 1956; Nisbett and Gordon, 1967). But personality factors also interact with particular states of the individual. For instance, ideological preconditioning, e.g. religion, allows the individual to counter subsequent indoctrinations of ideology with his own. Little experimental evidence is forthcoming, but dogmatism is often connected with authoritarianism.

One can, however, induce anxiety about the issue as in fear appeals. This leads to resistance, for by attaching anxiety to a given issue, individuals will subsequently avoid further exposure to the message and thus be less influenced. This was seen in the Janis and Feshbach (1953) study mentioned in Chapter 6, where strong fear appeals reduced communication effectiveness when evoking a high degree of emotional tension without adequately satisfying the need for reassurance.

Similarly, if one induced aggressiveness towards others, there is an increase in resistance to influence. Also, if an individual is given success experience, it enhances his resistance to subsequent social influence attempts (Kelman, 1953), even when the success experience is quite different to the influence task. But why does resistance occur when no pretraining or specific arousal of states is initiated – as certainly happens in everyday life? One attempt at an answer comes from Brehm (1966) in terms of *reactance*. Psychological reactance is seen as a motivational state that operates in opposition to inducing forces e.g. a persuasive communication.

It is assumed that 'when an individual's freedom to engage in a particular behaviour is eliminated or threatened with elimination, a motivation directed towards the re-establishment of the threatened freedom' is set up. In attitudes, it is assumed that an individual values a freedom to adopt certain attitudes and any force used to get him to adopt a particular attitude is seen as a threat to that freedom. Thus, the more he values the freedom, and the more force is exercised to make him adopt a particular attitude, the greater the amount of reactance and conversely the greater the striving of the individual to move away from the position he feels forced to adopt.

Attitudinal freedom consists of freedom to seek information or suspend judgement, and any premature pressure to decide on an issue will tend to result in avoidance of that decision; and pressure to adopt a particular stance will tend to produce increased interest in information supporting the opposing stance.

There are two distinguishable sources of the importance of freedom to adopt one's own position. Firstly, a feeling of competence the individual has in feeling that he can make a meaningful choice in the dimension in question. Secondly, the actual difference he finds between positions once he has time to study them – which is self-explanatory. Thus reactance and resistance may occur when, other things being equal, a threat to the freedom of choice is perceived. In a persuasive communication, there is always pressure to adopt a particular stance, yet reactance does not necessarily occur. It seems that in order to delineate the parameters under which reactance operates, one must at least know how the individual perceives the situation and how much he values his freedom to choose. Incidentally, many advertisers have seen the danger of appearing to threaten the customers' freedom of choice (see F6). This is why the soft sell has come more into fashion recently.

Like so many of the theories discussed one feels that the greatest weight lies in the phrase 'all other things being equal', which of course they rarely are. At any given point in any persuasive situation one can see the operation of personality factors, belief systems, motivational states and situational variables, all of which determine the manner in which the individual perceives the situation and thus responds. All of the theories have implications for clarifying the hierarchy in which these factors operate, but most of them fail to make exact predictions in a given situation. McGuire is, perhaps, an exception with his rigorous and methodical investigation, but then he confines himself to a specific type of situation rather than to give a general approach (cf. Rokeach).

Many factors are thus operating in a persuasive situation and, in summary, it appears that combinations of some or all of them improve resistance. It is unsure whether one could even distinguish the *most* important variable but the present chapter has attempted to give an overview of just some of the approaches which must come into consideration.

10
Functional approaches to attitude maintainance and change: relationship to psychoanalytic and learning theories

Throughout almost all areas of psychology, and indeed in many other subjects, both psychoanalytic and learning theory concepts have been utilized. In some cases these concepts are used formally to denote complete adherence to a particular viewpoint or framework and one can predict the direction of the discussion, literature and so on from one's knowledge of the theoretical superstructure. However, the language from both these major theoretical approaches has also been assimilated into general usage, and it is only rarely that no mention is made in postulates of such things as 'ego-defences' (see D3) or 'reinforcement' (see A3). All of psychology appears to be imbued with the residues of these monolithic and contradictory approaches. This present chapter examines functional attitude theories and the manner in which the language or the formal structure of these viewpoints underlies them. Thus we have, in Sarnoff's theory, a formal exposition of psychoanalytic theory. However, the majority of the functional theorists discussed here (i.e. Smith, Bruner and White; Katz) borrow language and assumptions from both doctrines whilst managing to reconcile them within one theory. Kelman is seen as slightly apart from the other functional theorists in that he concentrates solely on attitude change which is somewhat different to Katz's formulation.

Smith, Bruner and White (1956) have asked the question 'of what use to a man are his opinions?', and this question would appear to epitomize the central focus of the functional theories. It may be somewhat unfortunate that the answer supplied by such theorists takes the form of a list of needs and functions which are served by any one opinion or attitude. This is a very dangerous approach in some ways – one can see that, like McDougall's drives (see D2), one can always add on a new function every time a new attitude is uncovered or expressed. However, Katz (1960) has suggested three aspects of functional theories which make them useful in any conceptualization of attitudes. Firstly, he asserts that one advantage of functional theories is that they herald a step in the direction of a more *phenomenological* approach. That is to say that any stimulus can only be understood within the idiosyncratic context provided by each individual's own personality. We might add that although this may be a more realistic approach, pragmatically it seems to point to the impossibility of prediction as it seems unlikely that one could in fact define all these idiosyncrasies.

Secondly, Katz feels that by recognizing the various different functions of attitudes one can avoid oversimplification in the form of attributing a *single cause* to given types of attitudes. Katz, in his third point, contends that functional theories have an advantage in that they recognize the complex motivational source of behaviour and thus allow specification of the *conditions* under which given types of attitudes will change. It is unclear whether he means in relationship to individuals or in relationship to types of attitudes across individuals. Hopefully this point will be clarified later.

Kiesler, Collins and Miller (1969) also point out some of the useful aspects of functional theorists. One of their uses is that they take a position about the relationship between attitudes and other aspects of human behaviour. These theories perceive man as striving towards goals and analyses attitudes in terms of how much they facilitate the attainment of these goals. Such goals are evident from the behaviour of the individual and other facets of the personality. These goals, if they can be listed, not only provide a useful description but also operate as powerful empirical predictors. If this list can be combined with information about how an individual realizes those goals, then we have a useful description of that person. Again we must emphasize that whilst we feel in sympathy with this approach, the usefulness of any ideographic description is in question, especially when considering effects of mass communication, e.g. advertising and so on. It would seem, in fairness, that if this approach were plausible it may be most useful in individual therapy but becomes possible but unmanageable when dealing with more than one person. In a therapeutic situation, in agreement with Katz, it can be seen that knowledge of the functions that support opinions or attitudes provides useful information on how they are maintained. To discover the best way to modify them requires knowledge about why they are held presently or why they have changed in the past.

Many functional theories in psychology are essentially a typology or taxonomy of the needs that a particular set of behaviours fulfil, but the theories we shall be considering are somewhat more sophisticated, and attempt at specification of the antecedents and consequences of the functions in order to allow prediction and explanation within the theory. Smith, Bruner and White and Katz, list four major functions of attitudes. Both theories overlap and differ in that they disagree to a great extent on how attitudes are to be categorized. This clash of categories points to one of the flaws in the functional approach, in that it illustrates the arbitrary nature of any suggested functional boundary.

Katz

We will firstly look at Katz's (Katz, 1960; Katz and Stotland, 1959) definition of the four functions and show later how they are related to Smith, Bruner and White's.

1. *The instrumental, adjustive or utilitarian function.*
The first function recognizes the need in individuals to strive for and maximize the rewards in their external environment and to minimize the penalties. This is obviously a function which is fulfilled in most children's behaviour, and is one of the earliest to develop. Thus the child forms favourable attitudes to those objects which satisfy his needs and unfavourable ones to those which punish or thwart his needs. Katz emphasizes the points that it is the attitudinal *object* which is utilitarian, not the attitude itself. It is in discussing this function that Katz uses behaviour theory language; objects are seen as being *associated* with success or failure and thus associated with the achievement of positively valenced goals or with avoidance. Gradually, an individual will develop a posi-

tive attitude towards objects, and this is associated with an 'approach habit' towards these objects which serve a utilitarian function. Likewise, the individual develops a negative attitude and hence an 'avoidance habit' towards those objects which thwart his needs. These learned responses presumably are seen as obeying the laws of behavioural learning theory (see A3), and Katz sees these learned responses as the attitudes themselves. Coupled with these responses is an evaluative affect (i.e. the emotional component) which is also viewed as attitudinal. Katz does not exactly specify how these affective attitudes are acquired, but presumably it is in the terms either of 'operant' or 'classical' conditioning (Skinner, 1953).

Let us illustrate this with an example. Consider a child who is feeling hungry. He approaches a dish (conditioned stimulus) in which there is some food (unconditioned stimulus). This food then makes him feel sick (unconditioned response). After this has occurred a few times, the dish acquires the power to elicit the now conditioned response. That is, the mere sight of the dish is enough to make the child feel sick.

In the case of operant or instrumental conditioning (see Ch. 4), consider the same child who plays cooperatively with his younger brother. By doing this he receives a great deal of praise and attention from his mother. Thus, because praise and attention fulfils a need, the younger brother is seen as a utilitarian object by which to gain such satisfaction. Therefore, with sufficient reinforcement, the brother will acquire a positive evaluative affect as far as the elder is concerned.

Having thus acquired the attitudes associated with utilitarian objects, Katz gives the conditions under which such attitudes will be firstly aroused and secondly changed. The arousal of attitudes follows logically from the above discussion. One condition is the activation of the relevant need state, i.e. make the above child hungry and his attitudes associated with food will be aroused. Another condition is the arousal *via* cues that are associated with the attitude object and have associated with them favourable or unfavourable feelings. Thus a political candidate who defends motherhood and the family is attempting to arouse the positive reaction that many people associate with their mothers.

The conditions for change are quite similar in that by depriving the individual of the need which the object serves, or creating new needs, one can change the associated attitudes.

Likewise if the contingencies of punishment and reward are changed, or if new emphasis is placed on better paths for need satisfaction, the same change results.

The second major function is that of ego defence, and is the function that is most closely related to psychoanalytic thinking. This occurs when the individual attempts to protect himself from seeing basic truths about himself or the realities of the external world. As Katz (1960) has stated: 'Freudian psychology and Neo-Freudian thinking have been preoccupied with this type of motivation and its outcomes'. Incidentally, this subsection could also be categorized as the psychoanalytic theory of attitudes and will be discussed in more formal terms when considering Sarnoff's approach later. Whilst Katz's view of the ego-defensive function *is* basically psychoanalytic, its social psychological elaboration has its foundations more in the literature on prejudice, in that concentration is focussed on attitudes, about, for example, minorities. Ego-defensive attitudes may be aroused by internal or external threat, frustrating events, appeals to or the build-up of repressed impulses, and suggestions by authoritarian sources. Since these attitudes often employ displacement of aggression from the originally frustrating event onto some other, remoter, target, they are often difficult to change. However, change can occur through the removal of threat in a supportive environment (e.g. therapeutically), or by appeals that give information concerning the maladaptive aspects of the attitude whilst not threatening the individual at all. Some ego-defensive attitudes are aroused by the build-up of tension within an individual and this can be reduced by a cathartic release of his feelings, although this resolution is often only temporary and does not actually change the attitude involved. Additionally, Katz and his colleagues (McClintock, 1958; Stotland, Katz and Patchen, 1959) have explored the possibility that one can change ego-defensive attitudes by guiding the individual into some kind of insight into his own defensive mechanisms, as long as no threat is perceived by the individual in doing so.

The *third function* has been categorized by Katz as the *knowledge function* and is based on the individual's need to maintain a stable, organized and meaningful structure of the world in order to prevent chaos. This is done by having standards or frames of reference by which to judge events or objects, *etc.* Attitudes are seen as supplying such standards, and attitudes that develop or maintain cognitive consistency are obviously relevant. Such attitudes are generally elicited when some problem arises which cannot be solved without the information associated with the attitude. Such attitudes are of necessity changed when the existing attitude proves inadequate to deal with new situations either due to new and discrepant information or to a change in the environmental conditions, or, finally, because more meaningful information has been gathered.

This function is far less detailed than the ego-defensive function and has little experimental data connected with it. It appears to be probably the weakest aspect of all of Katz's theory and allows for few differential predictions for operations of the knowledge function.

The fourth and final function which Katz delineated is *the value expressive function*, which reflects the importance of the so-called 'ego psychology' in current psychoanalytic thought. This function has three main aspects to it: (a) it gives positive expression to an individual's central values and his self-identity. (b) it facilitates the definition of the individual's self-concept (for instance, a teenager will adopt the habits, dress and mannerisms of his peer group in order to define himself as one of that group and establish his status as a teenager). (c) If an individual comes into contact with a new group either by chance or on purpose, he will often adopt and internalize the values of that group, and their expression serves to help him relate to the group. Katz sees individuals as gaining satisfaction from expressing themselves and being able to reflect their values, beliefs and self-image. This self-image or concept in the adult is moulded mainly by social forces i.e. socialization, identification with reference groups *or* conformity to norms. In order to modify the attitudes with the reflection of the self-image, the propagandist must understand the social antecedents. The connected attitudes are likely to be aroused if something in the stimulus situation exists to cue the individual that an aspect of his self-image is relevant or when, in the immediate past, some thwarting of the individual's needs for expressive behaviour has occurred. To change these attitudes, Katz suggests, one must either create a degree of dissatisfaction within the individual with regards to his self-image, or attempt to show the individual that the specific attitude is at variance with some more central belief.

There appears to be relatively little experimental work specifically designed to test Katz's theory and in what data there is there tends to be many discrepancies. The data that is provided leaves much to be desired if it is to be seen as an empirical foundation for this functional theory, in that those hypotheses which have been tested are not unique to a functional theory of attitude change. For example, the notion of conformity and ego-defensive bases for prejudice has long been a part of the prejudice literature (Adorno, Frenkel-Brunswick, Levinson and Sanford 1950).

We will postpone further evaluation of Katz's theory until we have briefly discussed Smith, Bruner and White's approach, as many of the criticisms are appropriate to both.

Smith, Bruner and White (1956)

The above authors also postulate four functions of attitudes. Firstly, they consider the *social adjustment* function, in which the usefulness of an attitude is seen in establishing a social relationship. Thus one relates to reference groups by holding opinions expressed by that group. In this way they focus on the utilitarian function of the *attitude per se* in contradistinction to Katz's focus on the utilitarian nature of the *object.* This social adjustive function can take the form of expressing the need to be autonomous (paradoxically, through identifying with a reference group), or by indulging in hostility towards others by holding opinions contrary to the prevailing belief.

Secondly, the function of *externalization* is discussed. That is, when a person responds to an external event in a way that is distorted by unresolved internal conflicts. This is somewhat analogous to a psychoanalytic process and occurs in the following way. Covert strivings within the individual influence selective perception in that they create a predisposition to perceive this striving in an object (like the ego-defence known as projection). Hence, attitudes towards this object are influenced by the attitudes towards the inner strivings, allowing externalization of the conflict. These attitudes are also influenced by the preferred adjustive strategies of the individual and ones in which the individual has had past successes. Of course, the amount and importance of externalization will differ according to the individual.

Thirdly, the function of *object appraisal* is suggested. Whereas Katz stresses the tendency for individuals to impose a consistent structure on their environment as in the consistency theories, the above authors concentrate on the adaptive function which attitudes serve in meeting the day to day problems of life. That is to say, 'attitudes aid us in classifying for action the objects of the environment, and make appropriate response tendencies available for coping with these objects'. (Smith, Bruner & White, 1966, p. 41). This function is nearer Katz's utilitarian function than his knowledge function. However, both the knowledge function and object appraisal are both closely related to the Behaviour Theory concept of stimulus generalization (see A3).

Finally, we have the fourth function, that of the *quality of expressiveness*. In this category, Smith, Bruner and White diverge from the strictly functional approach in that they discuss the expressive *nature* rather than the *function* of attitudes. This category refers to the individual's style of operating. It is not connected to any need within the individual to express himself but rather to the way in which his opinions reflect the deeper pattern of his life. The authors explicitly reject the notion of an expressive need, and assert that the expressive aspect of attitudes does not perform any function for the rest of the personality.

From the above, one can see how the functional theories so far discussed have much in common both with learning theory and psychoanalytic theory. Whilst reading the originals, it is quite interesting to note the swing from one conceptual terminology to another. Concepts such as 'ego-defence', and 'unresolved conflicts' are intermingled with those of 'reinforcement contingencies' and 'stimulus generalization' in a way that can become confusing when trying to integrate all you have read.

In criticizing the above approaches, we will concentrate on Katz's theory as it is spelled out in greater detail and makes specific predictions for quantitative studies of attitude change. However, the criticisms are applicable to the other functional theory discussed, and to a greater or lesser extent to the theories of Kelman and Sarnoff considered in a separate section whilst still being included under the heading of 'functional theories'.

It is obvious from the exposition given so far that in order to change an attitude one must know which function it fulfils. Thus it is an idiographic approach, in that the same attitude can serve different functions for different individuals. Hence, it is powerless to predict attitude change unless we have a precise measure of the individual's characteristics. This is perhaps the foremost requirement and the most striking lack in functional theories i.e. a technology for assessing the function of attitudes. Little headway has been made and there has been hardly any attempt – notable exceptions being Adorno's F-scale, and Sarnoff's work (discussed later). In practical terms rather than logical ones, individual difference theories are always going to be difficult. The operational procedure must of necessity be time-consuming and expensive.

Different aspects of the theories have been subjected to detailed treatment by other theories. Thus the instrumental function has been dealt with by S-R or behaviourist theories of attitude, the knowledge function by consistency theorists and the ego-defensive function by psychoanalytic theories. Only the value-expressive function remains novel, and this is the very function which has little experimental evidence associated with it. Therefore, because of the very breadth of Katz's theory it tends to make few new predictions not accounted for by other theories. Himmelfarb and Eagley (1974) have suggested that the best way to consider this approach is as an attempt to integrate ideas of learning, consistency, psychoanalytic and value theories. However, they contend that even if this were done well, it is not particularly valid to draw them together by postulating separate *functions*. It would be more valid to see the separate schools of thought as emphasizing different aspects of the same underlying psychological *process*. It is difficult to ascertain whether the functions are as separate as the theorists suggest. They could easily imply and underlie each other in terms of a central need reduction with different approaches focussing on certain determinants of the process.

Another evaluation which should be brought to bear on any theory is the amount of hypotheses which are specific and clearly testable. Most of the unusual and specific predictions are associated with the psychoanalytic thinking behind the ego-defensive function of which more will be said later. Relatively few testable hypotheses are connected with the other functions, and there remains no specification of conditions under which the possibilities apply. Empirical tests of hypotheses will continue to be difficult when the functions are couched in such general terms, in that individual differences can always account for more variance to an outcome than environmental or situational factors. Unfortunately, this very issue relates to one of the fundamental propositions that Katz asserts when he argues that need systems fall into specific rank order in terms of their urgency. The generality of the functions and the resulting attitudes are a pervasive and unfortunate quality of all functional theories.

Katz and his colleagues have succeeded, however, in applying psychological concepts to a wide variety of social phenomena. But, except in the ego-defensive function, they have failed on the whole to delineate the conceptual boundaries of their theoretical terms, nor provided guidelines for the operationalization for these terms.

Having referred more than once to Sarnoff's fuller exposition of the ego-defensive function of attitudes, it now seems apposite to consider his theory here.

Sarnoff's Psychoanalytic Theory (1960–62)

In this theory, Sarnoff attempts a detailed description of the implications of Freudian theory, specifically, in the area of attitudes and attitude change. Firstly, he discusses motives and conflicts. In this he defines a motive as 'an internally operative, tension-producing stimulus, which provokes an individual to act in such a way as to reduce the tension generated by it, and which is capable of being consciously experienced'. Thus, if two or more motives are activated at any given time, conflict must necessarily ensue. However, if the motives differ in their intensity, the stronger one will always be given priority. If, then, there is no discernible difference in their intensity, the manner of conflict resolution depends on whether the motives are associated with intolerable fear, and thus are consciously unacceptable. If this is the case, the individual may suppress perception of one of the motives or inhibit it whilst remaining conscious of it. If, though, the motives are unacceptable, it may be deferred by means of a defence mechanism.

Before discussing the actual role of attitudes in such

situations, it is best to understand what we mean by ego defences thus countering any confusion incurred later.

To both Freud and Sarnoff, the child learns perceptual and motor skills which help reduce motivational tension within the limitations of the environmental restraints. Thus a child learns to perceive and attract attention but avoid punishments. Hence, the resulting configuration is the ego which allows the child to seek or avoid the appropriate consequences. Frequently, the child is unable to behave so adaptively either because he has not learned the appropriate motor or perceptual skills or because he is unaware how to attain his goals (or avoid punishment). In such a case as this the ego may loose its perceptual function completely, or the tension may become so great that the child looses consciousness. To avoid these rather extreme consequences, the individual makes covert responses to the intolerable fear in order to preserve the ego's perceptual function. The responses may come in the form of ego defence, and function to eliminate from consciousness the fear motive and any other motive which is responsible for the arousal of fear. Such ego defences include projection, where hostile feelings seen in oneself are seen in people around you, or 'projected' on to them; repression, where suppression from recognition of some inacceptable impulse occurs; identification, where one assumes certain characteristics from other people onto oneself, and so on.

However, tension is not guaranteed to be reduced by these mechanisms and in order to reduce it, some other covert response must be made. These responses then take the form of symptoms of which Sarnoff (1960a) says 'a symptom is an overt, tension-reducing response whose relationship to an unconscious motive is not perceived by the individual'.

What then is the relationship of the above to our general theme of attitude maintenance and change? Sarnoff defines an attitude as 'a disposition to react favourably or unfavourably to a class of objects'. Since attitudes are inferred from overt responses and since overt responses are made to reduce tension generated by motives, one may assume that attitudes are developed in the process of making tension reducing responses to various classes of objects and are determined by the role those objects play in facilitating reduction of tension.

Thus attitudes are associated with both consciously acceptable and consciously unacceptable motives and we will discuss them separately.

Firstly, *consciously acceptable motives.* According to Sarnoff, objects of an individual's environment fall into two major classes. There are those to which he must have access and towards which he must make a specific overt response in order to reduce tension of a given motive. There are also those objects which facilitate or thwart the possibility of making the necessary specific overt responses either by blocking access or leading to specific goals.

In this way, if an individual's motives are acceptable to him, it should be possible to predict a variety of his attitudes towards objects in his environment. Consider a man who has acquired a high need for achievement (see D2). To reduce tension generated by this motive he must make specific overt responses under specific conditions. Thus, if he has accepted his motives, one would expect a favourable attitude towards such things as work conditions which allow him to make responses in which the criterion of achievement can be imposed. Favourable attitudes would also be forthcoming towards prizes and medals, which are explicit objects conected with achievement, and also towards those persons who provide the opportunity to make responses that reduce the tension of the achievement motive. Conversely, one would expect unfavourable attitudes towards conditions which preclude tension reducing responses, such as low pay, bad work conditions and so on.

Sarnoff continues with an example of reducing tension generated by an aggressive motive. Aggression is often provoked by those who thwart the individual, and can be reduced by hostile or combative responses. Since attitudes anticipate responses, the individual develops unfavourable attitudes towards those objects to which he must respond with hostile acts, favourable attitudes are developed towards those objects that facilitate the maximum reduction of the aggression motive. Thus if X was helped by Y to discredit X's rivals, X would develop a favourable attitude towards Y.

Even if all the motives in a particular motivational conflict are acceptable, the individual cannot respond in a way that will reduce all tension. In order to reduce maximum tension in one motive, responses to others must be kept in abeyance.

The postponement of concentrating on the other motives can be facilitated by inhibition or suppression. Such phenomena as duplicity and hypocrisy may involve just such a discrepancy between an individual's behaviour (from which an attitude is inferred) and his conscious and inhibited motives. Attitudes which are formed in this way are illustrated by the discrepancy between publicly and privately expressed attitudes (Katz and Schank, 1938). Both attitudes are valid in that they facilitate the making of responses to reduce tension. Public attitudes are more likely to express facilitation of inhibiting or suppressing responses to motives, that is, if the verbalized attitude implies tension-reducing responses that the individual believes will evoke disapproval, they will be inhibited in public. In private there is a perceived lack of punishing consequences, and this allows free expression of those responses which are maximally reductive of the motive he inhibits in public.

Let us now consider what happens when the motive is *consciously unacceptable* to the individual. Usually, ego defences are developed whose operations are not discernible to the individual, but which prevent him from becoming cognisant of the motives which have traumatic implications for him. Hence, because the individual is unaware of both the motive and the defence, the conceptual and functional relationship between an attitude is much more complicated in this case.

Sarnoff gives the example of two individuals. Individual A is a Southern American shopkeeper and has conflicting motives of democratic ideals and making money. The latter is stronger and the former is inhibited as he deliberately acts in an anti-Negro way to appease his neighbours. Individual B, on the other hand, displays identical expressions of anti-Negro hatred, but these may be a result of ego-defences preventing acknowledgement of unacceptable aggressive motives. By means of projection, he may attribute that motive to Negroes and hence be spared the unpleasantness of recognizing it in himself.

Since individuals' consciously unacceptable motives cannot be predicted from manifest attitudes, Sarnoff gives two conditions to be fulfilled before a precise determination of the functional relationship between attitudes and motives can be attempted. Firstly, one must postulate which combination of consciously unacceptable motives and ego defences might account for the particular overt response from which the attitude is inferred. Secondly, the relationship between that combination and the attitude must be demonstrated empirically.

This approach seems quite sound, however, most of these demonstrations take the form of correlations (following Adorno *et al*, 1950), in that responses to attitude scales are correlated with responses to personality scales, projective lists or interviews. The reliability and validity of some attitude scales are questionable; those of personality scales are highly dubious; and reliability and validity from projective tests are practically nonexistent (see D3). The research is reviewed in Insko (1967) but most of it is inconclusive and ambiguous, when it is not directly contradictory. The drawbacks and difficulties of testing empirically any of Freudian theory is notorious and has been discussed elsewhere. It is not within the scope of this chapter to evaluate the theory very rigorously, it is presented here to illustrate the major functional theory that adheres to Freudian theory, language and principles.

We now turn to Kelman's theory. This theory differs from all the functional theories discussed in that the whole theory is built on the processes of attitude change. The other theorists concentrated on attitudes with relatively little emphasis on attitude change *per se*. In contrast to most other attitude change theories of the 1950s and 1960s, he is more concerned with the social psychological relationships than with the underlying psychological processes. Kelman does not talk about 'needs' that are satisfied, or 'functions' that attitudes or attitude change may serve. However, he does share one important goal with the other theorists, in that his theory clearly implies that knowledge of how an attitude was acquired is the key to knowing how to change it effectively. He also maintains the idiographic stance in that he contends that the same attitude may have developed in two different people by two different processes, and hence the methods of change will be different. As an attitude change formulation, Kelman's theory focusses specifically on the nature of the relationship of the message recipient to the source of the communication. Kelman distinguishes three sources of opinion change: *compliance*, *identification* and *internalization*. These differ in the motivational significance of the individual's relationship to the influencing agent, that is in the differing types of social integration that they represent. Another difference in the processes lies in whether the change occurs at a superficial level or at a deeper level which involves lasting effects on the individual's role relationships or values. Let us first consider *compliance*. This can be said to have occurred when an individual accepts influence because he hopes for a favourable reaction from another group or individual. He does not adopt the attitude because he believes in it, but in order to gain favoured specific rewards/punishments. Satisfaction from compliance is due to the social effect of accepting influence (Kelman, 1958), and the amount of attitude change depends on the control of rewards and punishments. However, once compliance occurs, the behavioural change will only be in effect when under surveillance by the influencing agent.

The second process is that of *identification*. This occurs when an individual accepts influence because he wants to establish or maintain what Kelman describes as 'a satisfying self-defining relationship to another person or group'. This can be achieved by classical identification where one individual takes over the role of another, or by a reciprocal role relationship. In this case, the individual believes in the responses he adopts but the specific context is more or less irrelevant, as the individual adopts the behaviour because it is associated with the desired relationship. The satisfaction gained from this is due to the mere act of conforming. For example, if a student wishes to be noticed he must identify with his role in relation to a tutor, and this will involve adopting the necessary responses (e.g. listening attentively, talking intelligently in seminars); but the *content* of such responses is irrelevant as long as it maintains the desired relationship.

The third process, *internalization*, occurs when an individual accepts influence because the content of the induced behaviour is intrinsically rewarding, and is congruent with the individual's existing value system. The behaviour is integrated with the existing values and the satisfaction comes from the content. The amount of attitude change produced depends on the prepotency of the response which is advocated. Once adopted, the induced behaviour will be performed under conditions of relevance of the issue regardless of salience or surveillance.

Kelman has formalized his theory by specifying several

antecedents and consequents of each process. These antecedents include specification of the crucial source attributes. Thus *means control* (the power over rewards and punishments) is crucial to compliance, *attractiveness* (in that it means a relationship is desirable) is necessary for identification; and *credibility* (ability to make perceived valid statements) is necessary for internalization.

In 1959 Kelman tested this model by manipulating the source of the influencing agent's power and assessed opinion change under varying degrees of control by the influencing agent. The results were consistent with the hypothesis – that means control elicits compliance, attractiveness elicits identification, and credibility elicits internalization.

While the experimental evidence is scarce, Kelman's theory contributes to an understanding of the conditions that influence the maintenance and stability of opinion change. Kelman has extended his model to extend to such things as integration of the individual into the national system (Kelman, 1969), influence processes in psychotherapy (Kelman 1963) and, most recently, to the linkage of the influence recipient to the broader social system (Kelman, 1971). However, it is difficult to see to what extent these three processes constitute a theory. Kiesler, Collins and Miller (1969) have stated that 'the theory at best is a set of three laws; at worst it is a set of three definitions'. One may ask if the antecedents are mutually exclusive, or if indeed the three processes are interchangeable. Kelman's theory is much more specific than the other functional theories, which makes it easier to draw new hypotheses from it. However, there is little follow up research, and more is needed before a full evaluation is appropriate.

In summary, it seems that although the functional approaches have generated some interesting ideas, they are severely limited both practically and empirically. That attitudes serve functions and are thus needed by the individual is a theme echoed in both the Introduction and the concluding chapter. The way in which we need them and the functions they serve have not, as yet, been clearly defined – the proffered definitions being arbitrary and backed up with relatively little evidence.

Finally, the present chapter has attempted to show the close ties that the discussed theories have with psychoanalytic and learning language and theory.

11 Conclusion: the link between values, attitudes and behaviour

In this last chapter we shall attempt to summarize some of the findings arising from the book and also look at the questions posed in Chapter 1.

We can place the topics to be discussed under three headings.

(a) Is there any relationship between values, attitudes and behaviour?
(b) Do we need the concepts of values and attitudes to understand the motives and behaviour of people?
(c) What are the best approaches for effecting change with special emphasis on behavioural change.

We mentioned in Chapter 3 that each attitude is said to contain a cognitive, affective and tendency-to-act component, and that there is a positive relationship between these components. By knowing the direction and strength of one of the components, one should be able to predict the same for the other two. We also found, especially in the works of Rokeach and Rosenberg, that differences in value orientations are good predictors of specific attitudes. It therefore appears that values and attitudes have intrapersonal consistency and that they are persistent over time. The relationship between these concepts and behaviour is far more tenuous. It is difficult to predict specific behaviour by knowing someone's values and attitudes. It is however much easier to predict from someone's intentional behaviour what his attitude and relevant values are towards the object. Eagly and Himmelfarb (1974) in discussing this question quote Cook and Selltiz (1964), who noted that additional factors may intervene between the value-attitude orientation and subsequent behaviour. Firstly, there may be other motives, or personal dispositions which clash with the *behavioural* expression. Secondly, there may be situational factors, such as norms of the appropriateness of the behaviour, and the expectations of others, which are relevant and may be crucial as to whether the value-attitude orientation will be expressed in action.

Abelson (1972) discusses the above question at length. He quotes Smith (1969) who argues that it would be 'naive to count very much on such a tendency ... to bring people's behaviour into line with their moral principles. The whole history of human frailty scores against such a result.' Abelson looking at the question as a cultural phenomenon (which we pass on to our children who imitate us), writes 'we are well trained and very good at finding reasons for what we do, but not very good at doing what we find reasons for'. (We often tell children 'do what I tell you', forgetting that they observe and copy what we *do*.) By looking at ways which Abelson suggests may strengthen the value-attitude-behaviour link, we can indirectly observe why he thinks the relationship is so tenuous. One method which he suggests is through 'encouragement cues', which will increase the probability that one will express one's attitudes behaviourally. He suggests three kinds of encouragement cues. (1) social modelling; (2) self-perception as a doer; and (3) unusual emotional investment. He quotes studies which indicate the powerful effect of modelling in a variety of circumstances, ranging from volunteering for an experiment (Rosenbaum, 1956) to helping a girl to change a flat tyre. His second encouragement is by planting the idea into a person that he is the kind of person who is a 'doer'. He quotes some evidence (McArthur, Kiesler and Cook, 1969) which shows this to be effective.

Thirdly, Abelson has in mind that linking the required behaviour to a strong feeling which is consonant with the behaviour, should flood out any situational restraint, or the fear of looking foolish by engaging in that behaviour. He is really concerned with the jump from 'theory to practice' translating one's dispositions into 'reality'. What he is suggesting is how to overcome some constraint inhibiting the response. If we look at his suggestions, the second refers to a change in self-perception, the third a stronger mobilization of affect to overcome the inhibition. The first suggestion may be the most powerful. The 'model' translates intention into action and thus validates for the observer the correctness of this response. Because behaviour is less revocable than private thoughts and intentions, its validation may be necessary for the correctness in one's own eyes and in the eyes of others. In addition to the suggestion of Abelson, one may consider other ways of strengthening the value-attitude-behaviour relationship. One, that we have already come across in Chapter 6 is by 'facilitating' the behaviour. Leventhal, Singer and Jones (1965) found that even when subjects' attitudes to the need for tetanus shots had changed and when they had also expressed an intention to have them, the actual behaviour change depended on spelling out specific forms of action of how and when to get the shots. Perhaps there is an additional intertia factor which has to be overcome to energize action, as Abelson hinted at in his second suggestion above.

We have found in various chapters different orientations, and emphases, on the importance of values and attitudes. We are talking here of values and attitudes to external objects and people and not towards the self. We may believe that values and attitudes are important to us, and even strict behaviourists may secretly share this belief. Is there evidence that this is more than a cultural fashion? We feel that one ought to make a clear distinction between patterns arising in childhood and those arising later. If we concentrate on the acquisition of behaviour and the affective component of the attitude only we get positive (approach) behaviour accompanied with 'liking', or negative (avoidance) behaviour with 'dislike' of the object. Developmentally, there is little doubt that conditioning and modelling establish behavioural patterns with their emotional counterpart. These 'associations' are established and maintained by external stimuli, the child *reacts*. It appears however, and here we are using Kelman's categorization as a developmental process, that when these are internalized they are integrated into other behaviour patterns *and* cognitions and values of the person. These values and attitudes then take on an autonomous quality which make the variety of responses into a meaningful whole which we perceive as the 'I'. We will then as adolescents and adults acquire attitudes and behaviour patterns to new objects as they fit in with our existing picture of ourselves. We suggest that this stage comes with maturity as the perception of oneself as a fixed point of acting on the environment as a person is developed. The extreme changes during adolescence, appear less in behaviour irregularities, but rather in changes in values and attitudes which the growing person can claim as his own, and according to which he can then direct his behaviour as a unique individual. That people believe that they have gone to war, or made other sacrifices in defence of their values and attitudes, can only mean that they consider this as important for their self-perception. We already suggested in Chapter 1 that just as man needs an ordered environment within which he can operate efficiently, he also wants an *ordered self*, from which he can operate as a person *on* the environment.

This approach is in line with that of Zimbardo (1969). His book consists of sixteen experimental studies and reviews concerned with the effect of dissonance arousal on specific motives. The latter range from biological drives like hunger and thirst to personal and social motives like the need to avoid failure and control of aggression. What he in effect shows is that, when a person voluntarily commits himself to a response which is dissonant with his motivation (e.g. to fast when he is already hungry), this commitment will bring about a change in his motivation. This change ('I am not hungry') will make the motivation consonant with the cognition which follows from his commitment ('I can't be hungry'). The emphasis in the papers is to show that acting from free choice, transforms the motivation and behaviour to make the 'environment' fit one's self perception of a free agent.

What are the best methods of effecting change? Much of the book has been concerned with this topic, especially Chapter 8. As we pointed out at the beginning of this chapter, we cannot normally expect behaviour to follow values and attitudes, but we can infer values and attitudes from intentional behaviour. It should follow therefore that a change in the other two will best be effected by behaviour change. This chain effect, if it occurs, will only happen when the new behaviour is maintained and internalized. If it has arisen under circumstances of conformity and compliance the new behaviour would not persist, as the subjects in the Asch experiment (see p. 22) reverted to their earlier 'correct' perception when removed from the group. Nor would the behavioural act change the corresponding values and attitudes. Will maintenance of the new behaviour also lead to new values and attitudes? There is sufficient evidence from Festinger and his associates that behaviour change is a good predictor for attitude change. The *reason* why this should be so is still unresolved. For Bem at one extreme attitudes and values are only subjective inferences from any given behaviour. For the more cognitively orientated psychologist it is possibly due to the notion that cognitive disequilibrium is more easily resolved by changing an attitude than by explaining an action which contradicts the previously held attitude. What nevertheless seems to unite approaches as varied as those of Festinger, Hovland and Bem, is the underlying picture of man's perception of himself. On discussing the Hovland group's work in Chapter 6 we concluded with the central notion of ego-involvement in a particular issue. Festinger's research is not any more about two cognitions which appear to be contradictory. As Abelson (1968) has put it: 'Thus, at the very heart of dissonance theory; where it makes its clearest and neatest predictions, we are not dealing with just two cognitions; rather, we are usually dealing with the self-concept and cognitions about some behaviour. If dissonance exists it is because the individual's behaviour is inconsistent with his self-concept.' Even if we follow Bem, we can only deduce certain attitudes and values from behaviour, because an observer seeing the voluntary action assumes that if the person chose to do so he must have a positive attitude towards the object or person. There is thus a common assumption of how a person wants to perceive himself and to be perceived by others.

We have stressed the need in man for both order and freedom; we have argued that experimental research from diverse orientations appear to confirm this. For many researchers it was the assumption underlying their work. We felt the need to spell it out. Mischel (1968) and Argyle and Little (1972) have shown that situational variables are more important to account for variable behaviour than are personality factors. Our intention has been not to restore personality factors, with their emphasis on individual differences, but rather to claim importance for the person in his perception of himself and of his environment.

References and Name Index

The numbers in italics following each entry refer to page numbers within this book. Asterisked references are especially recommended for further reading.

Abelson, R. (1959) Modes of resolution of belief dilemmas. *Journal of Conflict Resolutions 3*: 343. *92*

*Abelson, R. (1968) Psychological implications. In R Abelson, G. Aronson, W. J. McGuire, T. M. Newcomb, M. J. Rosenberg, and P. H. Tannenbaum (eds) *Theories of Cognitive Consistency: A Source Book.* Chicago: Rand McNally. *133*

*Abelson, R. (1972) Are attitudes necessary? In B. T. King and E. McGinnies (eds) *Attitudes, Conflict and Social Change.* New York: Academic Press. *13, 130*

Abelson, R. and Rosenberg, M. (1958) Symbolic psycho-logic: a model of attitudinal cognition. *Behavioural Science 3*: 1–13. *86, 94*

*Adorno, J. W., Frenkel-Brunswick, E., Levinson, D. J. and Sandford, R. N. (1953) *The Authoritarian Personality.* New York: Harper and Row. *41, 110, 119, 126*

*Allport, G. W. (1961) *Pattern and Growth in Personality.* New York: Holt, Rinehart and Winston. *18, 21*

Allport, G. W., Vernon, P. G., and Linzey, G. (1951) *Study of Values.* Boston: Houghton-Mifflin. *21*

Anderson, N. H. (1968) Likeableness rating of 555 personality trait words. *Journal of Personality and Social Psychology 9*: 272–9. *109*

Anderson, N. H. (1971) Information integration and attitude change. *Psychological Review 78*: 171–206. *109*

Anderson, L. and McGuire, W. J. (1968) Prior reassurance of group consensus as a factor in producing resistance to persuasion. *Sociometry 28*: 44–56. *107*

Argyle M. and Little, B. R. (1972) Do personality traits apply to social behaviour? *Journal for the Theory of Social Behaviour 2*: 1–35. *133*

*Aronson, E. (1972) *The Social Animal*. San Francisco: W. H. Freeman. *51*

*Aronson E. and Carlsmith, J. M. (1968) Experimentation in social psychology. In G. Lindzey and E. Aronson (eds) *A Handbook of Social Psychology*, Vol. II. Reading, Mass.: Addison-Wesley. *71*

Asch, G. E. (1956) Studies in independence and conformity: 1, A minority of one against a unanimous majority. *Psychological Monograph 70* (9) *Whole No. 416*. *22*

Bandura, A. (1969) Social learning theory of identifactory processes. In D. A. Goshin (ed.) *The Handbook of Socialisation Theory and Research*. Chicago: Rand McNally. *45*

*Bandura, A. and Walters, R. H. (1963) *Social Learning and Personality Development*. New York: Holt, Rinehart and Winston. *45*

Bem, D. J. (1965) An experimental analysis of self-persuasion. *Journal of Experimental Social Psychology 1*: 199–218. *81, 95*

Bem, D. J. and McConnell, H. R. (1970) Testing the self perception explanation of dissonance phenomena. On the salience of pre-manipulation attitudes. *Journal of Personality and Social Psychology 14*: 23–31. *97*

*Berkowitz, L. (1961) Anti-semitism, judgemental processes and displacement of hostility. *Journal of Abnormal and Social Psychology 62*: 210–15. *53*

Bogardus, E. S. (1925) Measuring social distance. *Journal of Applied Sociology 9*: 216–26. *34*

Bramel, D. (1968) Dissonance, expectation and the self. In R. P. Abelson *et al.* (eds) *Theories of Cognitive Consistency: A Sourcebook*. Chicago: Rand McNally. *68, 88*

Brock, T. C. and Becker, L. A. (1965) Ineffectiveness of 'overheard' counter-propaganda. *Journal of Personality and Social Psychology 2*: 654–60. *60*

*Brehm, W. J. (1966) *A Theory of Psychological Reactance*. New York: Academic Press. *74, 110*

*Brehm, W. J. and Cohen, A. (1962) *Explanation in Cognitive Dissonance*. New York: Wiley. *64, 74, 81, 83*

*Brown, R. (1965) *Social Psychology*. New York: Free Press.

Campbell, A., Converse, P. C., Miller, W. G. and Stokes, D. G. (1960) *The American Voter*. New York: Wiley. *29*

Cohen, A. R. (1959) Communication discrepancy and attitude change. A dissonance theory approach. *Journal of Personality 27*: 386–96. *110*

Cohen, A. R. (1964) *Attitude Change and Social Influence*. New York: Basic Books. *12*

Collins, B. G. and Hoyt, M. G. (1972) Personal responsibility for consequences. An integration and extension of the 'forced compliance' literature. *Journal of Experimental Social Psychology 16*: 199–206. *69, 82*

Cook, S. W. and Selltiz, C. A. (1964) A multiple indicator approach to attitude measurement. *Psychological Bulletin 62*: 36–55. *130*

Cooper, J., and Worschel, A. (1970) Role of undesired consequences in arousing cognitive dissonance. *Journal of Personality and Social Psychology. 16*: 199–206. *82, 84*

Crespi, L. P. (1945) Public opinion against conscientious objectors. III. Intensity of social rejection in stereotype and attitude. *Journal of Psychology 19*: 251–76. *34*

Deutsch, M. and Gerard, H. (1955) A study of normative and informational social influences upon individual judgement. *Journal of Abnormal and Social Psychology 51*: 629–56. *100*

Elms, A. and Janis, I. (1965) Counter-norm attitudes induced by consonant versus dissonant conditions of role-playing. *Journal of Experimental Research in Personality 1*: 50–60. *80, 84*

Eysenck, H. J. (1947) Primary social attitudes. 1. The organisation and measurement of social attitudes. *International Journal of Opinion Attitude Research I*: 49–84. *48*

Eysenck, H. J. (1970) *Psychology is About People*. London: Allen Lane Press. *48*

Festinger, L. (1957) *A Theory of Cognitive Dissonance*. Stanford: Stanford University Press. *72, 78*

Festinger, L. (ed.) (1964) *Conflict, Decision and Dissonance*. Stanford: Stanford University Press. *13, 78*

Festinger, L. (1964a) Behavioural support for opinion change. *Public Opinion Quarterly 28*: 404–17. *78*

*Festinger, L. (1968) Foreword to Greenwald, A. G., Breck, T. G. and Ostrom, T. M. (eds) *Psychological Foundations of Attitudes*. New York: Academic Press. *83*

Festinger, L. and Carlsmith, J. (1959) Cognitive consequences of forced compliances. *Journal of Abnormal and Social Psychology 58*: 203–10. *76, 80*

Festinger, L., Schachter, S. and Back, K. (1950) *Social Pressures in Informal Groups*. New York: Harper and Row. *47*

Hilgard, E. R. (1965) *Hypnotic Susceptibility*. New York: Brace. *70*

*Himmelfarb, S. (1974) Resistance to persuasion induced by information integration. In S. Himmelfarb and A. Eagley (eds) *Readings in Attitude Change*. New York: John Wiley. *68, 83, 109, 121, 129*

Hollander, C. P. (1971) *Principles and Methods of Social Psychology*. Oxford: Oxford University Press. *22*

Hovland, C. I. (ed.) (1957) *The Order of Presentation in Persuasion*. New Haven: Yale University Press. *65, 68*

Hovland, C. I., Harvey, O. J. and Sherif, M. (1957) Assimilation and contrast effects in reactions to communication and attitude change. *Journal of Abnormal and Social Psychology 55*: 244–52. *67*

Hovland, C. I., Lumsdaine, A. A. and Sheffield, F. D. (1949) *Experiments in Mass Communication*. Princeton: Princeton University Press. *64*

Hovland, C. I. and Mandell, W. (1952) An experimental comparison of conclusion-drawing by the communicator and the audience. *Journal of Abnormal and Social Psychology 47*: 581–8. *66*

Hovland, C. I. and Weiss, W. (1951) The influence of source-

credibility on communication effectiveness. *Public Opinion Quarterly 15*: 635–50. *58*
*Insko, C. I. (1967) *Theories of Attitude Change*. New York: Appleton-Century-Crofts. *72, 77, 107, 126*
Janis, I. L. and Feshbach, S. (1963) Effects of fear arousing communications. *Journal of Abnormal and Social Psychology 48*: 78–92. *62, 110*
Janis, I. L. and Field, P. (1959) Sex differences and personality factors related to persuasibility. In C. I. Hovland and I. L. Janis (eds) *Personality and Persuasibility*. New Haven: Yale University Press. *51, 69*
Janis, I. L. and Field, P. (1959) A behavioural assessment of personality consistency of individual differences. In C. I. Hovland and I. L. Janis (eds) *Personality and Persuasibility*. New Haven: Yale University Press. *70, 110*
Janis, I. L. and Gilmore, J. (1965) The influence of incentive conditions on the success of role-playing in modifying attitudes. *Journal of Personality and Social Psychology 1*: 17–27. *79, 80*
Johnson, H. H. and Scileppi, I. D. (1969) Effects of ego involvement conditions on attitude change to high and low credibility communications. *Journal of Personality and Social Psychology 13*: 31–6. *59*
Jones, E. E. and Gerard, H. B. (1967) *Foundation of Social Psychology*. New York: John Wiley. *17, 88*
Katz, D. (1960) The functional approach to the study of attitudes. *Public Opinion Quarterly 24*: 163–204. *114, 115, 117*
Katz D. and Schank, R. L. (1938) *Social Psychology*. New York: Harper. *125*
Katz, D. and Stotland, E. (1959) A preliminary statement to a theory of attitude change and structure. In S. Koch (ed.) *Psychology, A Study of Science*, Vol. 3. New York: McGraw-Hill. *20, 115*
Kelman, H. C. (1953) Attitude change as a function of response restriction. *Human Relations 6*: 185–214. *75, 79, 100, 110*
Kelman, H. C. (1958) Compliance, identification and internalisation. Three processes of attitude change. *Journal of Conflict Resolutions 2*: 51–60. *127*
Kelman, H. C. (1963) The role of the group in the induction of therapeutic change. *International Journal of Group Psychotherapy 13*: 399–432. *128*
Kelman, H. C. (1969) Patterns of personal involvement in the national system. A social psychological analysis of political legitimacy. In J. N. Rosenau (ed.) *International Politics and Foreign Policy* (2nd ed.). New York: Free Press. *128*
Kelman, H. C. (1971) *Social influence and the linkages between the individual and the social system. Further thoughts on the process of compliance, identification and internalisation.* Paper presented at the Albany Symposium on Power and Influences, State University of New York at Albany. *128*
Kelman, H. C. and Baron, R. H. (1974) Moral and hedonic dissonance. A functional analysis of the relationship between discrepant action

and attitude change. In S. Himmelfarb and A. Eagley (eds) *Readings in Attitude Change*. New York: John Wiley. *68, 82, 84*

Kelman, H. C. and Hovland, C. I. (1953) Reinstatement of the communicator in delayed measurement of opinion change. *Journal of Abnormal and Social Psychology 48*: 327–35. *59*

*Kelvin, P. (1969) *The Bases of Social Behaviour*. New York: Holt, Rinehart and Winston. *14*

*Kiesler, C. A., Collins, E. and Miller, N. (1969) *Attitude Change. A Critical Analysis of Theoretical Approaches*. New York: John Wiley. *114, 128*

King, B. T. and Janis, I. L. (1956) Comparison of the effectiveness of improvised versus non-improvised role-playing in producing opinion change. *Human Relations 9*: 177–84. *101*

Kretch, D., Crutchfield, R. A. and Ballachy, E. L. (1962) *Individual in Society: A Textbook of Social Psychology*. New York: McGraw-Hill. *29*

Lasswell, H. D. (1948) The structure and function of communication in society. In L. Bryson (ed.) *Communication of Ideas*. New York: Harper. *57*

Leventhal, H. (1969) Findings and theory in the study of fear communications. In L. Berkowitz (ed.) *Advances in Experimental Social Psychology*, Vol. 5. New York: Academic Press. *63*

Leventhal, H. R., Singer, P. and Jones, S. (1965) Effects of fear and specificity of recommendation upon attitudes and behaviour. *Journal of Personality and Social Psychology 2*: 20–9. *131*

Likert, R. (1932) A technique for the measurement of attitudes. *Archives of Psychology 140*. *32*

Lund, F. M. (1925) The psychology of belief. IV. The law of primacy in persuasion. *Journal of Abnormal and Social Psychology 20*: 183–91. *65*

Maslow, C., Yoselson, K. and London, M. (1971) Persuasiveness of confidence expressed via language and body language. *British Journal of Social and Clinical Psychology 10*: 234–40. *61*

Mausner, B. and Block, B. L. (1957) A study of additivity of variables affecting the social interaction. *Journal of Abnormal and Social Psychology 54*: 250–6. *71*

McArthur, L. A., Kiesler, C. A. and Cook, B. P. (1969) Acting on an attitude as a function of self-percept and inequity. *Journal of Personality and Social Psychology 12*: 295–302. *130*

McCaulay, J. R. (1965) *A study of independent and assertive modes of producing resistance to persuasion derived from congruity and inoculation models*. Unpublished doctoral dissertation: University of Wisconsin. *109*

McClintock, C. G. (1958) Personality syndromes and attitude change. *Journal of Personality 26*: 479–593. *117*

McGuire, W. J. (1964) Inducing resistance to persuasion: some contemporary approaches. In L. Berkowitz (ed.) *Advances in Experimental Social Psychology*, Vol. 1. New York: Academic Press. *100, 101, 103, 107, 108*

McGuire, W. J. (1968) Personality and susceptibility to social influence. In E. Borgatta and W. W. Lambert (eds) *Handbook of Personality Theory and Research*, Vol. 3. Chicago: Rand McNally. *28, 29, 69*

*McGuire, W. J. (1969) The nature of attitude and attitude change. in Lindzey and Aronson (eds) *Handbook of Social Psychology*, Vol. 3. Reading, Mass.: Addison-Wesley. *57*

McGuire, W. J. and Papegeorgis, D. (1961) The relative efficacy of various types of prior belief defense in producing immunity against persuasion. *Journal of Abnormal and Social Psychology 62*: 327–37. *106*

Miller, N. (1965) Involvement and dogmatism as inhibitors of attitude change. *Journal of Experimental Social Psychology 1*: 121–32. *68*

Miller, N. and Bugelski, R. (1948) Minor studies in aggression: the influence of frustrations imposed by the in-group on attitudes expressed toward out-groups. *Journal of Psychology 25*: 437–42. *53*

Mills, J. and Jellison, J. M. (1967) Effect on opinion change of how desirable the communication is to the audience the communicator addressed. *Journal of Personality and Social Psychology 6*: 98–101. *60*

Mischel, W. (1968) *Personality and Assessment*. New York: John Wiley. *131*

Moreno, J. L. (1953) *Who Shall Survive?* (2nd ed.) New York: Beacon. *34*

Nisbett, R. E. and Gordon, A. (1967) Self-esteem and susceptibility to social influence. *Journal of Personality and Social Psychology. 5*: 268–76. *110*

Osgood, C., Suci, G., and Tannenbaum, P. (1957) *The Measurement of Meaning*. Urbana: University of Illinois Press. *29, 33, 90, 91*

Pettigrew, T. F. (1958) Personality and sociocultural factors in intergroup attitudes: a cross-national comparison. *Journal of Conflict Resolution 2*: 29–42. *54*

Pushkin, I. (1967) *A study of ethnic choice in the play of young children in three London districts*. Unpublished doctoral thesis, University of London. *35*

Rokeach, M. (1960) *The Open and Closed Mind*. New York: Basic Books. *41, 100, 102*

*Rokeach, M. (1967) referred to in Rokeach, M. (1973) *The Nature of Human Values*. New York: Free Press. *23, 80, 85, 86, 89*

Rokeach, M. and Cochrane, R. (1972) Self-confrontation and confrontation with another as determinants of long term value change. *Journal of Applied Social Psychology, 2*: 293–5. *89*

Rokeach, M. and Mezei, L. (1966) Race and shared beliefs as factors in social choice. *Science, 151*: 167–72. *10*

Rosenbaum, M. E. (1956) The effects of stimulus and background factors on the volunteering response. *Journal of Abnormal Social Psychology 53*: 118–21. *130*

Rosenberg, M. J. (1956) Cognitive structure of attitudinal affect.

Journal of Abnormal Social Psychology 53: 367–72. *93, 101*
Rosenberg, M. J. (1960) Cognitive reorganization in response to the hypnotic reversal of attitudinal affect. *Journal of Personality 28*: 39–63. *29*
Ruechelle, R. D. (1958) An experimental study of audience recognition of emotional and intellectual appeals in persuasion. *Speech Monographs 25*: 251–79. *62*
Sarnoff, I. (1960a) Psychoanalytic theory and social attitudes. *Public Opinion Quarterly 24*: 251–79. *122, 123*
Schachter, S. and Hall, R. L. (1952) Group-derived restraints and audience persuasion. *Human Relations 5*: 379–406. *101*
Schachter, S. and Singer, J. E. (1962) Cognitive, social and psychological determinants of emotional state. *Psychological Review 69*: 379–99. *95*
Secord, P. F. and Backman, C. W. (1974) *Social Psychology*. New York: McGraw-Hill. *47, 48, 55*
Sherif, M. (1951) Experimental study of intergroup relations In J. H. Rohwer and M. Sherif (eds) *Social Psychology at the Crossroads*. New York: Harper and Row. *47, 51*
Sherif, M. (1966) *In Common Predicament: Social psychology of Intergroup Conflict and Cooperation*. Boston: Houghton–Mifflin. *47*
Sherif, M., Harvey, O. J., White, B. J., Hood, W. R. and Sherif, C. W. (1961) *Intergroup Conflict and Cooperation; The Robbers' Cave Experiment*. Norman Institute of Group Relations, University of Oklahoma. *47, 55*
Sherif, M. and Hovland, C. I. (1961) *Social Judgement: Assimilation and Contrast in Communication and Attitude Change*. New Haven: Yale University Press. *67*
Sherif, M. and Sherif, C. W. (1953) *Groups in Harmony and Tension*. New York: Harper and Row. *47*
Sherif, C. W., Sherif, M. and Nebergall, R. C. (1965) *Attitudes and Attitude Change: The Social Judgement-Involvement Approach*. Philadelphia: Saunders. *68*
Skinner, B. F. (1953) *Science and Human Behaviour*. New York: MacMillan. *116*
*Skinner, B. F. (1957) *Verbal Behaviour*. New York: Appleton-Century-Crofts. *95*
*Skinner, B. F. (1971) *Beyond Freedom and Dignity*. New York: Knopf. *16*
Smith, H. B. (1969) *Some Thoughts on the Legitimation of Evil: Social Psychology and Human Values*. Chicago: Aldine. *130*
Smith, H. B., Bruner, J. S. and White, R. W. (1956) *Opinions and Personality*. New York: John Wiley. *29, 113, 119, 120*
Star, S. A., Williams, R. M. and Struffer, S. A. (1958) Negro infantry platoons in white companies. In Maccoby, E., Newcomb, T. M. and Hartley, E. (eds) *Readings in Social Psychology* (3rd ed.). New York: Holt, Rinehart and Winston. *55*
Stotland, E., Katz, D. and Patchen, M. (1957) The reduction of

prejudice through the arousal of self-insight. *Journal of Personality 27*: 507–31. *117*
Tannenbaum, P. H. (1956) Initial attitude towards source and concept as factors in attitude change through communication. *Public Opinion Quarterly 20*: 413–35. *109*
Tannenbaum, P. H. (1966) Mediated generalization of attitude change via the principle of congruity. *Journal of Personality and Social Psychology 3*: 493–9. *108*
Tannenbaum, P. H. (1967) The congruity principle revisited. Studies in the reduction induction and generalization of persuasion. In L. Berkowitz (ed.) *Advances in Experimental Social Psychology*, Vol. 3. New York: Academic Press. *108*
Taylor, J. A. (1953) A personality scale of manifest anxiety. *Journal of Abnormal and Social Psychology 48*: 285–90. *36*
Thurstone, L. L. and Chase, E. J. (1929) *The Measurement of Attitude*. Chicago: University Chicago Press. *31*
Triandis, H. C. (1971) *Attitudes and Attitude Change*. New York: Wiley. *34*
Valins, S. (1966) Cognitive effects of false heart-rate feedback. *Journal of Personality and Social Psychology 4*: 400–8. *95*
Vaughan, G. M. and Mangan, G. L. (1963) Conformity to group pressure in relation to the value of task material. *Journal of Abnormal and Social Psychology 66*: 179–83. *22*
Vidulich, R. N. and Kresunick, I. P. (1966) Racial attitudes and emotional response to visual representations of the Negro. *Journal of Social Psychology 68*: 85–93. *29*
Walster, E., Aronson, E. and Abrahams, D. (1966) On increasing the persuasiveness of a low prestige communicator, *Journal of Experimental Social Psychology 2*: 325–42. *60*
Walster, E. and Festinger, L. (1962) The effectiveness of 'overheard' persuasive communications. *Journal of Abnormal and Social Psychology 65*: 395–402. *60*
Weatherley, D. (1961) Anti-semitism and expression of fantasy aggression. *Journal of Abnormal and Social Psychology 62*: 454–7. *53*
Zajonc, R. (1960) The process of cognitive learning in communication. *Journal of Abnormal and Social Psychology 61*: 159–67. *101*
Zimbardo, P. G. (1960) Involvement and communication discrepancy as determinants of opinion conformity. *Journal of Abnormal and Social Psychology 60*: 86–94. *68*
*Zimbardo, P. G. (1969) *The Cognitive Control of Motivation*. New York: Scott, Freeman. *14, 132*

Subject Index

GLASGOW UNIVERSITY